JOSEPH BORO

The Olympian's

The Story of Olympic, Titanic, and Britannic

BORO BOOKS

First published by Boro Books 2025

Copyright © 2025 by Joseph Boro

All rights reserved. No part of this publication may be reproduced, stored or transmitted in any form or by any means, electronic, mechanical, photocopying, recording, scanning, or otherwise without written permission from the publisher. It is illegal to copy this book, post it to a website, or distribute it by any other means without permission.

Joseph Boro asserts the moral right to be identified as the author of this work.

Joseph Boro has no responsibility for the persistence or accuracy of URLs for external or third-party Internet Websites referred to in this publication and does not guarantee that any content on such Websites is, or will remain, accurate or appropriate.

Designations used by companies to distinguish their products are often claimed as trademarks. All brand names and product names used in this book and on its cover are trade names, service marks, trademarks and registered trademarks of their respective owners. The publishers and the book are not associated with any product or vendor mentioned in this book. None of the companies referenced within the book have endorsed the book.

For My Papa

Contents

Acknowledgments

I want to thank thank my family during this writing process. I couldn't have done this without their support.

Introduction

The story of the Titanic is often told with a brief mention that she was the second of three sister ships, but then quickly delves into the infamous disaster that has come to define her legacy. And understandably so. The sinking of the Titanic was not just a tragedy but the deadliest peacetime maritime disaster for nearly eighty years. It shocked the world, capturing the imaginations of generations and compelling widespread reforms in maritime safety. Yet, in focusing on the Titanic's catastrophe, we often lose sight of the fact that she was merely one part of a trio. These ships were conceived together, each playing a role in the grand vision of the White Star Line. While Titanic's ill-fated maiden voyage is the most widely discussed, it's crucial to remember that she was the middle child in a class of ships designed to be revolutionary in their time.

Mentions of the Titanic's sister ships, Olympic and Britannic, occasionally appear, but the conversation inevitably gravitates back to the Titanic's tragic sinking. It's not difficult to understand why; the scale of the disaster, the romanticism of the era, and the heart-wrenching stories of the passengers make it an irresistible narrative. Yet, in this collective fixation on the Titanic, we overlook a remarkable contrast. The R.M.S. Olympic, the class's namesake and prototype, is the only one of the trio to fully complete her intended service. The Titanic is forever known for her collision with an iceberg and her dramatic plunge into the depths of the Atlantic. Meanwhile, Olympic, often affectionately nicknamed "Old Reliable," survived multiple collisions, saw combat during World War I, and sailed successfully for over two decades. In layman's terms, Olympic hit nearly everything—and survived.

There is something undeniably fascinating about the fact that these ships, constructed over a century ago, continue to occupy a space in our cultural consciousness. They were created by a company that no longer exists, in a world that is vastly different from our own, and yet, they remain iconic. Why? Why are these ships, essentially just machines designed to transport people across oceans, still such a potent symbol? The answer lies in the stories behind the steel hulls, in the human drama that unfolded on and around them. These ships were not merely tools; they were stages where life, death, survival, and heroism played out on a grand scale.

The tale of the Titanic is one of profound tragedy. It's a story of loss, of dreams cut short, and of what might have been if only the crew had acted a few moments faster, if only there had been enough lifeboats, if only the iceberg had been spotted a little sooner. The Titanic's story is dominated by these heartbreaking "what ifs," leaving an indelible mark on history. The Britannic, though less well-known, also met a tragic end, but her story is different. Converted into a hospital ship during World War I, she was struck by a mine and sank in the Aegean Sea. Though the loss of life was significantly lower, Britannic's story is intertwined with the war, making it not just a tale of tragedy, but also of the conflict and chaos of the times.

Then there's the Olympic. Olympic's story, unlike those of her sisters, is one of triumph, endurance, and resilience. She had her share of near-misses and brushes with disaster, but Olympic prevailed. During World War I, she was converted into a troopship and earned the nickname "Old Reliable" after successfully transporting tens of thousands of soldiers across dangerous waters. In 1918, she even rammed and sank a German U-boat, adding a rare moment of combat glory to her service record. After the war, Olympic returned to civilian life, continuing to sail across the Atlantic for more than a decade before being retired in 1935. Her longevity and service make her the triumphant sibling, a ship that faced adversity and emerged victorious time and time again.

The stories of these three ships—Titanic, Britannic, and Olympic—should be seen as parts of a larger narrative, each contributing its own chapter to maritime history. The Titanic's tragedy doesn't stand alone; it's part of a family history, one of loss and survival. Olympic, as the lone sister to complete her career, serves as a "what if" for her fallen siblings. What might have happened if Titanic had survived her maiden voyage? What kind of stories would have been told about her decades later? What if Britannic hadn't met with a mine in the Aegean Sea? Olympic's story gives us a glimpse of what could have been, a chance to imagine a different outcome for the White Star Line's great trio.

Yet, Olympic's story is more than just a mirror for her sisters. She has her own rich history of triumph over adversity, of serving through war and peace. It's a tale of a ship that, while sharing the DNA of her more famous sibling, made her mark on the world through survival and endurance, not disaster. Olympic's career, in a way, complements the stories of the Titanic and Britannic. She is the reminder that not all ships are doomed to tragedy, that resilience and success can be just as compelling as loss.

Each of these ships deserves to have their stories told in full. While Titanic's disaster has rightfully earned its place in history, Olympic's achievements should not be overshadowed. Together, the three sisters form a tapestry of human ambition, triumph, tragedy, and resilience. It is through their collective stories that we can truly understand the legacy of the Titanic class. And in doing so, we give Olympic her rightful place as the ship that endured when others fell, the last of her line to stand as a testament to what might have been. This is Olympic's story, and it deserves to be told.

1

Chapter 1

Arms Race

Any story about the RMS *Olympic* must also, inevitably, be a story about the RMS *Titanic*. The two are so deeply entwined—built side by side, envisioned as twins in a grander trio—that to separate them from the start is to miss the broader context of their creation. They share a common origin: conceived by the same company, constructed in the same shipyard, and born out of the same national ambitions. It is only after their respective launches that their fates begin to diverge. Yet, to truly understand either vessel's place in history, one must begin with the story they shared.

It is the early 20th century. The age of steam and steel has transformed the oceans into arenas of national competition. Naval supremacy was not just about military might—it was about prestige, industrial prowess, and economic dominance. Nowhere was this more evident than in the growing rivalry between Great Britain and Germany.[1] The two nations were locked in a naval arms race, each striving to outdo the other not only with dreadnoughts and cruisers, but also with civilian ocean liners that symbolized modernity and luxury.

In Britain, the civilian maritime competition was fiercest between two long-established companies: the Cunard Line and the White Star Line. Cunard had long been the standard-bearer of British maritime excellence, known for its fast and efficient transatlantic service. But White Star, under the ownership of the American financier J.P. Morgan's International Mercantile Marine Co. (IMM), was not content to follow. They sought not just to match Cunard, but to redefine luxury sea travel altogether.

Although they were rivals, Cunard and White Star's fates were intertwined by the pressures of national expectation and commercial ambition. Cunard had already launched the *Lusitania* and *Mauretania*, two groundbreaking ships known for their speed and engineering. In response, White Star envisioned a new class of ships—grander, more spacious, and more opulent than anything that had come before. Thus, the *Olympic*-class liners were born: RMS *Olympic*, RMS *Titanic*, and eventually RMS *Britannic*.

The *Olympic* and *Titanic* were constructed nearly simultaneously at the Harland & Wolff shipyard in Belfast, Northern Ireland. They shared the same dimensions, similar layouts, and many design elements. The *Olympic* launched first in 1910 and entered service in 1911. The *Titanic* followed shortly after, embarking on her ill-fated maiden voyage in April 1912.

---

[1] https://www.iwm.org.uk/history/the-naval-race-between-britain-and-germany-before-the-first-world-war

To tell the story of one without the other is to leave it half-finished. For a complete understanding of their design, purpose, and place in history, their shared origin must first be acknowledged. Only then can their individual stories—so different in outcome—be properly appreciated.

* * *

Founded in 1840 by Sir Samuel Cunard[2] as the British and North American Royal Mail Steam-Packet Company, the Cunard Line initially operated paddle steamers for transatlantic crossings. For thirty years[3], the company maintained its dominance by holding the prestigious Blue Riband—the informal accolade awarded to the passenger liner with the fastest transatlantic crossing. This achievement was not only a point of pride for the company but also a matter of national prestige for Great Britain.

However, by the latter half of the 19th century, Cunard began to face increasing competition from both domestic and foreign rivals, including the emerging White Star Line. Concurrently, advances in marine engineering were transforming the shipping industry. New propulsion technologies, such as the transition from paddle wheels to screw propellers and the shift from iron to steel hulls, promised greater speed, reliability, and capacity. Despite benefiting from these technological trends,

---

[2] https://www.cunard.com/en-us/cunard-stories/180-years-of-cunard#

[3] https://www.royalparks.org.uk/visit/parks/brompton-cemetery/famous-graves-burials/sir-samuel-cunard-1787-1865

Cunard began to lose its competitive edge.

Sir Samuel Cunard, BBC Hulton Picture Library

In 1879, facing mounting financial difficulties, the company was reorganized as a publicly traded entity and officially adopted the name Cunard Line.[4] As part of this reorganization, Cunard commissioned its first steel-hulled passenger liner, marking a strategic shift to modernize its fleet and challenge its competitors more effectively.

From this point forward, Cunard committed itself to a dual focus on speed and luxury, seeking to outmatch both the German Inman Line and the White Star Line. Nevertheless, these efforts initially proved insufficient. In 1897[5], the Inman Line (then operating as part of the American-owned International Navigation Company) claimed the Blue Riband with the SS *Kaiser Wilhelm der Grosse*, signaling a new era of German supremacy in transatlantic travel. This loss of prestige deeply unsettled Cunard and the British maritime establishment.

In response, plans were laid to reclaim Cunard's former dominance. With substantial support from the British government, including subsidies and loans granted in exchange for the ships' availability as armed merchant cruisers in wartime, Cunard began work in 1904 on two revolutionary vessels: *RMS Lusitania* and *RMS Mauretania*. These ships were not only designed to be the largest in the world but also the fastest, incorporating cutting-edge turbine propulsion systems.

Both ships were launched in 1907, June for *Lusitania*[6], and September for *Mauretania*[7], just three months apart. Their debut marked a turning point in ocean liner history. Of the

---

[4] https://web.archive.org/web/20221128141848/https://shiplife.org/cruise-lines/cunard-line/

[5] https://www.greatoceanliners.com/blue-riband

[6] https://www.iwm.org.uk/history/18-minutes-that-shocked-the-world#:~:text=The%20Lusitania%20was%20launched%20on,as%20an%20armed%20auxiliary%20cruiser.

[7] https://www.historytoday.com/archive/launch-mauretania

two, *Mauretania* proved the faster, capturing the Blue Riband for the fastest eastbound transatlantic crossing in 1907, and for the fastest westbound crossing in 1909. She held both records for an impressive twenty years, becoming a symbol of British technological excellence and maritime supremacy.

Cunard's triumph did not go unnoticed. Its rivals took heed, particularly White Star Line under the leadership of J. Bruce Ismay. Recognizing that his company could not compete on speed, Ismay chose a different strategy—he would compete on scale and luxury. This decision would ultimately lead to the construction of the *Olympic*-class liners: *Olympic*, *Titanic*, and *Britannic*—vessels intended to redefine oceanic travel not through record-breaking velocity, but through unprecedented size, comfort, and grandeur.

* * *

Founded in 1845 by John Pilkington and Henry Wilson, the White Star Line initially focused its operations on routes between Britain and Australia.[8] This strategic choice was largely influenced by the Australian gold rush, which had triggered a surge in emigration to the former penal colony. Unlike its eventual rival, Cunard, whose operations were centered on transatlantic crossings, White Star sought to capitalize on the colonial migration boom.

The young line ended up chartering several clipper ships in order to run the Australia route. So as to stand out among

---

[8] https://www.whitestarhistory.com/history

the competition, safety was emphasized in regards to White Star's fleet, though the opposite focus tended to be the reality.[9] This would actually cause White Star several problems, as they couldn't live up to their promises.

In a twist of either irony or coincidence, one of the ships chartered for the Australia route was a clipper by the name of the R.M.S *Tayleur*, the largest sailing vessel ever built in England.[10] On January 19, 1854, the *Tayleur* departed Liverpool for Melbourne, Australia on her maiden voyage. What could go wrong, went wrong, and fast.[11] This ranged from non-functional compasses due to the ships iron hull, the rudder being too small for the ship's tonnage, faulty rigging, bad weather, and a partially untrained crew of whom some did not speak English. All this together resulted in the *Tayleur* running against rocks off the coast of Dublin on January 21, 1854. Of the 652 passengers and crew onboard, only 280 survived. Of this number, only three women and 3 children survived.[12]

Although a disaster, White Star used this as reason to purchase its own ships, and manages to counter back, having won contracts to carry the mail. Unfortunately this contract requires said mail to be delivered within a certain time period, or face penalties, of which White Star failed to perform as contracted. In September 1856, White Star Lone looses its contract to carry the mail. In January 1857, John Pilkington

---

9 https://www.titanicandco.com/whitestarline/wslindex.php

10 http://www.wslmf.org/discover/chronology/

11 https://www.liverpool.ac.uk/~cmi/books/emigrant/tayleur.html#:~:text= Tayleur%20left%20Liverpool%20on%2019,year%2Dold%20Captain%20 John%20Noble.

12 https://coastmonkey.ie/rms-tayleur/

becomes disillusioned and leaves the company, mainly over his partners business practices.

Over the next few years, Henry Wilson takes out loans and overextends the company financially so as to buy or charter new ships, and chase the current hot route. In October 1867, the Royal Bank of Liverpool, which had had been providing loans to White Star Line failed.[13] This forced White Star Line to have to pay back its debt of £527,000, which forced the company into bankruptcy.

In 1867, the name and house flag of the bankrupt company was bought by Thomas Henry Ismay for £1,000.[14] He acquired the firm's name with the intention of repositioning its commercial focus, and to capitalize on its goodwill with the public.[15] Backed financially by Gustav Schwab, Ismay began pivoting the White Star Line away from the Australia-bound routes in favor of the more profitable transatlantic passage to New York. While some historians argue that this shift was orchestrated primarily to secure contracts for Schwab's nephew's shipbuilding firm, Harland and Wolff (co-founded by Gustav Wolff), others maintain that Ismay had always intended to target the lucrative North Atlantic market and merely saw the alliance as an expedient opportunity. this doesn't really make much sense however, as part of the new partnership stipulated that Harland and Wolff would build ships exclusively for White Star Line, in exchange for a share of the

---

[13] https://travelwithintent.com/2014/12/09/white-star-line-titanic-liverpool-belfast/

[14] https://travelwithintent.com/2014/12/09/white-star-line-titanic-liverpool-belfast/

[15] https://mollybrown.org/history-of-the-white-star-line/

Thomas Henry Ismay, 1899; Image Courtesy of WikiCommons

revenues generated from the vessels' operation.[16] As a result, the line commissioned six new ships for transatlantic service—known collectively as the *Oceanic*-class—which utilized both sail and steam power.[17]

The *Oceanic*-class vessels began entering service in early 1871, though not without difficulty. The launch of the *RMS Oceanic* was marred by mechanical failures during her maiden voyage, incidents which attracted unfavorable press and damaged public perception. Nevertheless, White Star gradually recovered, culminating in the attainment of the Blue Riband for the fastest eastbound transatlantic crossing in January 1873.

However, misfortune soon struck again. In March 1873, the *RMS Atlantic*, another *Oceanic*-class ship, ran aground on rocks off the coast of Nova Scotia while attempting an unscheduled coal stop near Halifax.[18] The tragedy claimed 585 lives out of 952 on board, making it the deadliest civilian maritime disaster in the Atlantic at that time. Investigations attributed the calamity to the captain's unfamiliarity with the area and the unnecessary nature of a refueling stop.

Despite the enormity of this loss, the White Star Line not only endured but continued to grow. Its ships, renowned for balancing speed with unprecedented luxury, prompted rivals like Cunard and the Inman Line to respond with their own ambitious new vessels. In turn, White Star remained competitive by commissioning even larger and more powerful ships with each successive generation. During this period, the company

---

[16] https://oceanlinersmagazine.com/2021/01/17/white-star-line-sold-1000/

[17] https://www.titanicandco.com/whitestarline/oceanicclass.html

[18] https://www.ssatlantic.com/ssatlantic/history/

also expanded into new markets through partnerships and subsidiaries that operated in the Indian and Pacific Oceans, though these ventures were not branded under the White Star name.[19]

Technological evolution further reshaped maritime strategy. The reliance on sails diminished, and by the late 19th century, White Star had transitioned entirely to steam-powered ships. With escalating competition and rising construction costs, financial sustainability became a growing concern. In 1887, Thomas Ismay struck an agreement with the British government: in exchange for state subsidies, White Star vessels would be made available for military use in the event of war.[20] This arrangement proved beneficial, with ships eventually serving as troop transports during the Second Boer War.

Crucially, White Star was not alone in forging such arrangements. Cunard had entered into a similar partnership, and the two companies remained in fierce competition—continually attempting to outclass each other in size, speed, and luxury.

Thomas Ismay, however, did not live to witness the peak of his company's evolution. He died on November 23, 1899, at the age of 62[21], following complications from gallstones and multiple unsuccessful surgeries. Leadership of the company passed to his son, Joseph Bruce Ismay, commonly referred to as J. Bruce Ismay.

Under J. Bruce Ismay's direction, White Star Line adopted a

---

[19] https://www.whitestarhistory.com/oceanic

[20] https://www.titanicandco.com/whitestarline/firstliners.html

[21] https://static1.squarespace.com/static/5c65dd81af46834afd07e40a/t/5ec56a642f7cfc3aa7da511c/1589996155309/lives+retold+ismay+thomas.pdf

new strategic focus. While previous decades had emphasized speed, Ismay shifted the company's priorities toward unparalleled scale and opulence. Though transatlantic speed records still held some value, they were no longer deemed essential to commercial success. Instead, Ismay envisioned vessels so grand in size and amenities that they would redefine maritime luxury.

Such ambitions, however, required substantial capital investment. Fortuitously, an opportunity arose that would not only solve this financial challenge but elevate White Star's position within the global shipping industry. In 1902, Ismay negotiated the sale of White Star Line to American financier J. Pierpont Morgan, who was in the process of consolidating a number of shipping companies into a new conglomerate. On October 1st of that year, White Star Line became a part of the International Mercantile Marine Company (IMM), a vast transatlantic enterprise under Morgan's control.[22]

---

[22] https://titanichistoricalsociety.org/international-mercantile-marine-company/

J. Bruce Ismay, 1912; image Courtesy Wiki Commons

Although J.P. Morgan owned IMM, day-to-day operations were entrusted to J. Bruce Ismay, who retained his position as president of White Star Line while simultaneously serving in a senior role within IMM. In this dual capacity, Ismay gained unprecedented influence and access to the resources necessary to realize his grand designs. There were rumors that the largest owner of White Star Line stock, William J Pirrie, had misgivings in regards to J. Bruce Ismay ability to run the company, and pushed for the sale as a result. But this has never been proven and seems odd when considering the fact that Ismay became head of IMM after the purchase.

* * *

The early years of IMM were marked by commercial prosperity, fueled in part by high rates of immigration from Europe to the United States. Yet this period of growth would not last. The sinking of the *RMS Titanic* in 1912, a tragedy that deeply implicated both White Star and Ismay personally, marked the beginning of a prolonged decline. This was further exacerbated by the upheaval of World War I and the economic devastation of the Great Depression.

Still, prior to that pivotal disaster, Ismay had taken bold steps to secure White Star's dominance. At a dinner party in 1907, he proposed the construction of what would become the Olympic-class liners—three ships that would embody his vision for maritime supremacy. Among them was the *RMS Titanic*, a vessel whose name would become synonymous not only with grandeur, but also with one of the most infamous tragedies in maritime history.

2

Chapter 2

Design, Safety, & Construction

By 1907, J. Bruce Ismay—President of both the White Star Line and its parent company, the International Mercantile Marine (IMM)—found himself facing a critical challenge. Just a year earlier, White Star's chief rival, the Cunard Line, had launched the RMS *Lusitania*, a ship that not only captured the prestigious Blue Riband for the fastest Atlantic crossing, but also raised the bar for maritime luxury. Cunard wasn't done yet either; her twin sister ship, the *Mauretania*, was set to launch shortly, promising even greater speed and opulence.

These twin leviathans were a threat to White Star Line's long-established market niche. Though the company had largely given up the speed race in favor of luxury, Cunard's new ships were threatening to dominate both. Ismay recognized that to stay competitive, White Star would need to respond— not by matching speed, but by redefining the very concept of passenger travel.[23] In a private meeting that same year with financier and company owner J.P. Morgan, Ismay laid out his ambitious vision: a new class of ships that would outshine Cunard not in speed, but in size, comfort, and sheer grandeur.[24] Morgan, eager to expand IMM's prestige and returns, agreed.

Soon after, White Star Line commissioned its longtime part-ner, the Belfast-based shipbuilders Harland & Wolff, to bring Ismay's dream to life. The result would be one of the most iconic classes of passenger vessels ever conceived: the Olympic-class liners. The class would be named after its first ship, *Olympic*, and would eventually include the now-legendary *Titanic* and her slightly altered sister, *Britannic*.

There is some historical debate about who truly deserves the title of chief designer of these colossal ships. Official records credit Thomas Andrews, a rising star at Harland & Wolff, as the lead architect. However, many historians and maritime experts point to another figure who deserves equal—if not more—recognition: Alexander Montgomery Carlisle.

* * *

Born in 1854, Carlisle was the son of a schoolmaster and was by all accounts, a brilliant student. At the age of sixteen,

---

[23] https://rmstitanichistory.tripod.com/the-white-star-line.html

[24] https://www.history.co.uk/articles/titanics-sister-ships-olympic-class-ocean-liners

he began an apprenticeship at Harland & Wolff[25], a common practice in that era for promising young men and over the next several decades, he rose through the company ranks to become its Chief Draughtsman and later, Chief Designer. Known for his relentless work ethic and a nearly perfect attendance record, Carlisle was instrumental in laying out the foundational blueprints of the Olympic-class ships.

[25] https://www.titanicbelfast.com/history-of-titanic/titanic-stories/who-really-designed-the-titanic/

Alexander Carlisle; Image TitanicBelfast.com

It is now widely accepted that Carlisle was responsible for many of the early conceptual designs of both *Olympic* and *Titanic*, working alongside Harland & Wolff's leadership and White Star executives. Among his many contributions, he drew up the specifications for the ships' bulkheads, deck plans, and most controversially—their safety provisions.

So why, then, is Thomas Andrews so often remembered as the chief designer? The answer lies in Carlisle's abrupt and somewhat mysterious resignation and subsequent retirement from Harland & Wolff in 1910, just as construction on *Olympic* neared completion. Following his departure, Andrews stepped into the role of overseeing the project and would later be aboard *Titanic* during her ill-fated maiden voyage, where he tragically perished while helping passengers escape. Andrews's heroism and visibility in the disaster likely cemented his legacy in the public memory.

As for Carlisle's resignation, several theories emerged as for a reason, but the most compelling centers around a dispute with Ismay over lifeboat provisions. Carlisle had originally proposed outfitting each Olympic-class liner with at least forty-eight lifeboats—enough to accommodate every soul on board. Some sources suggest a minimum of thirty-two. Regardless of the precise number, it is clear Carlisle prioritized safety and compliance with the best standards of the time.

Ismay, however, had other priorities. He envisioned the upper decks—especially the boat deck—as areas of leisure and aesthetic refinement. He believed a promenade deck with unobstructed views would better serve the ship's image of opulence and modernity. Lifeboats, in his view, were excessive eyesores and unnecessary for a vessel considered virtually unsinkable. Carlisle's insistence on more lifeboats clashed with Ismay's vision, and with neither side yielding, the disagreement escalated.

Officially, Carlisle would retire in June 1910 due to a nervous breakdown following an argument, leaving a hole in the Belfast Shipping community, one that would not go unnoticed by the trades:

> "There was a general feeling of regret that Mr. A.M. Carlisle, who until the end of June had been for many years so closely associated with the chairman of the company in all the great projects of the firm, was not present, and the hope was expressed that the rest he is taking will restore him to his wonted vigour."[26]
> ~ Shipping world Magazine, 1910

By the letter of British maritime law at the time, both *Olympic* and *Titanic* — along with their yet-to-be-completed sister ship, *Britannic* — were required to carry only sixteen lifeboats. In practice, all three vessels exceeded this minimum and were designed to cary twenty, a modest surplus of four.[27] This compliance stemmed not from any forward-thinking design philosophy, but from outdated regulations that determined the required number of lifeboats based on a vessel's gross tonnage rather than the number of souls it could carry.

Though history would later judge this standard as tragically insufficient, it is worth noting that the *Olympic*-class ships

---

[26] https://www.encyclopedia-titanica.org/carlisle-retirement-separating-fact-from-fiction.html

[27] https://blogs.loc.gov/law/2012/04/failure-to-update-the-law-a-titanic-mistake/

adhered to every legal requirement of the time. Even with more passengers and crew than lifeboat space available, the White Star Line was not violating any law. In fact, in many ways, these ships marked a notable improvement over others of the era.

One could argue that overconfidence in the technological marvels of the time played a role in the limited number of lifeboats. The *Olympic*-class vessels were designed with numerous safety features considered advanced for their day. These included a double-bottom hull and a series of watertight bulkheads intended to slow the spread of flooding in the event of a hull breach. While the design didn't call for a full double hull initially, and the bulkheads only reached as far as D or E deck — roughly ten feet above the waterline — they were nevertheless considered a significant leap forward in shipbuilding.

It is commonly said that these ships were designed to be "unsinkable." In reality, neither *Titanic* nor her sister ships were ever officially described as such, or at least per Harland and Wolff that is.[28] They maintain the position that the term did not emerge until after *Olympic* collided with the Royal Navy cruiser *HMS Hawke* in 1911, and managed to return to port despite substantial damage. The idea is that the ship's robust construction inspired confidence, and the idea of the ships being unsinkable began to take root in public imagination. This claim however is proven false, when a White Star Line brochure from 1910[29] was found promoting that the ships were indeed designed to be unsinkable.

---

[28] https://www.historyonthenet.com/the-titanic-why-did-people-believe-titanic-was-unsinkable

[29] https://www.printwand.com/blog/how-unsinkable-marketing-campaign-led-titanic-disaster?srsltid=AfmBOoodUihQKZ8goi5u-YdORqingCdOfiYOwM3aOGNcvP9fWQyWrLDx

that the latter will make her maiden voyage July. 1911 ; and as far as it is possible to do so, these two wonder-ful vessels are designed to be unsinkable.

White Star Line Brochure 1910, image Courtesy PrintWand.com

Harland & Wolff also claims that the idea of the *Olympic* Class liners being unsinkable was fueled by a misquote from the shipbuilders, who originally stated that the vessels were "prac-tically unsinkable." They claim that over time, the qualifier was dropped, and that the phrase took on a life of its own, becoming a tragic irony following *Titanic*'s demise. This does paint Harland & Wolff as either liars, or poor record keepers, which would make them a poor source to cite either way, except when one has no choice.

* * *

Going to the other extreme, some claim that the *Olympic*-class ships were reckless in design, and that it was White Star Lines fault for there not being enough lifeboats. This however is not the case. In truth, the *Olympic*-class ships were not death traps. They met and in many ways exceeded the safety standards of their time. Designed with sixteen watertight compartments, these bulkheads were intended to keep the vessel afloat even if up to four compartments were breached. Unfortunately, the iceberg impact that doomed *Titanic* ruptured at least five. Moreover, the bulkheads did not extend high enough to prevent water from spilling over from one to the next — a critical flaw only fully recognized in hindsight.

Still, these safety features weren't without merit. The intent was for a damaged ship to remain afloat long enough for nearby vessels to assist in evacuation. Lifeboats, under this doctrine, were meant not to carry everyone at once but to shuttle people between ships. It was assumed that help would arrive in time — a belief that proved tragically optimistic in the North Atlantic.

The term "overbuilt" is often applied to the *Olympic*-class liners, and perhaps rightly so. At the time of their construction, they were the largest ocean-going vessels ever built. Though modest by today's cruise ship standards, *Olympic* and *Titanic* were marvels of engineering, opulence, and scale. As *Titanic* is described in Cameron's film — "the ship of dreams" — the title feels fitting.

Designed at the direction of J. Bruce Ismay, chairman of the White Star Line, the vessels aimed not only to be large but luxurious. In this, they succeeded spectacularly. The ships offered three distinct passenger classes, each physically separated and tailored to its own clientele, much like modern airline classes. Yet even among this familiar stratification,

Olympic and *Titanic* stood apart in what they offered.

Third class, for example, was significantly more accommodating than on most contemporary liners. Rather than crowded dormitories, passengers enjoyed cabins furnished with beds and storage trunks. A third-class ticket on *Titanic* cost around £7 — equivalent to roughly £400 today[30] — and included access to dedicated dining and smoking rooms, amenities almost unheard of in steerage at the time. Although only two baths were available, they did exist — a small but notable upgrade in third-class standards.

Second class offered even greater comfort, comparable to first-class accommodations on many other ships. Cabins featured wardrobes and private washbasins, and typically accommodated three passengers. Communal restrooms and bath facilities were standard early on but were later upgraded aboard *Olympic* during refits. Second-class passengers enjoyed their own dining saloon, smoking room, and even a library. The ship's band, technically second-class passengers themselves, would perform for these guests when not entertaining first class.

First class, however, was in a league of its own. Situated in the ship's superstructure to minimize vibrations — an issue that plagued rivals like *Lusitania* and *Mauretania* — first-class accommodations ranged from standard cabins to grand suites. Even the basic rooms came with foldaway washbasins, wardrobes, call buttons for stewards, electric lighting, and heaters — all state-of-the-art in 1912.

---

[30] https://www.cruisemummy.co.uk/titanic-ticket-prices/

Titanic Stateroom B-59, Courtesy of WikiCommons

The most elite accommodations were the parlor suites: multi-room apartments with private entrances, lavish furnishings, and even exclusive promenades. Only four existed per ship, two of which were "deluxe" with their own private deck space. While *Olympic* did not initially feature these promenades, they were added during a 1913 refit following *Titanic*'s sinking.

Other first-class amenities included a swimming pool, Turkish baths, a gymnasium, and elegantly decorated lounges. Despite Hollywood dramatizations, strict segregation existed between the classes. Passengers could not move freely between sections, even by invitation.

As for the crew, their quarters varied greatly depending on their role. Officers and senior stewards were stationed closer to the passengers they served, while most of the crew — stokers, trimmers, engineers — were housed near the ship's bottom decks alongside the third-class cabins. This was common practice, then and now, to keep working staff close to their duties and out of public view, albeit at the cost of noise and discomfort from the engines.

The power behind these ships came from a sophisticated engineering setup: two 15,000 horsepower reciprocating engines and a 16,000 horsepower low-pressure turbine, driving three propellers. These engines were fed by 29 coal-fired boilers, later converted to oil on *Olympic* in 1919. Altogether, they could generate up to 59,000 horsepower in emergencies.

All three *Olympic*-class ships were originally to be built to identical dimensions — 883 feet in length and 92 feet in width — though this would change in time. After *Titanic*'s sinking, both *Olympic* and the under-construction *Britannic* were retrofitted with significant safety enhancements. *Britannic* was widened during construction to accommodate a true double hull and gantry davits, giving her a distinct appearance. *Olympic*, already completed, underwent a 1913 refit that included installing an inner watertight skin, heightened bulkheads, and an additional compartment — though at the expense of interior space.[31]

One of the most consequential upgrades was to the lifeboat capacity: *Olympic*'s count rose from 20 to 68. However, due to her narrower beam, she could not adopt the gantry davits seen on *Britannic*, limiting how lifeboats could be launched.

In retrospect, the *Olympic*-class liners embodied both the triumphs and the blind spots of early 20th-century ship de-

---

[31] http://www.titanicology.com/Modifications_To_Olympic.html

sign. They were innovative, luxurious, and robust — but not invulnerable. Their story, especially that of *Titanic*, continues to fascinate and teach us, not only about engineering and safety but also about the human tendency to trust too deeply in progress without preparing for its limitations.

* * *

On December 16th, 1908, in the bustling industrial heart of Belfast, a significant moment in maritime history quietly unfolded.[32] At yard number 400, slipway 347, within the Harland & Wolff shipyard, the keel was laid for what would eventually become the *R.M.S. Olympic*, the first of the White Star Line's legendary *Olympic*-class ocean liners. At that time, the ship had no name—simply referred to as "Number 400"—a towering symbol of ambition, innovation, and the fierce competition of the North Atlantic passenger trade.

To accommodate the construction of these colossal vessels, Harland & Wolff undertook extensive modifications to its facilities. A brand-new construction area was purpose-built specifically for the project, capable of holding two of the three planned liners side-by-side—Olympic and her sister ship *Titanic*. This required the demolition of three existing slipways, which had previously been used for much smaller ships, marking a transformative evolution in the shipyard's capacity. The new gantry structure, designed by Sir William

---

[32] https://titanic-olympic.wixsite.com/luxury/post/3-things-the-most-res
ilient-people-do-every-day

Arrol & Co., was itself an engineering marvel, spanning over 840 feet in length and rising more than 220 feet high, allowing workers unprecedented access to every part of the vessel during construction.[33]

The concept for Olympic and her sisters had only recently been approved by White Star Line chairman J. Bruce Ismay in July 1908, following intense planning and collaboration with Harland & Wolff's chief designer, Alexander Carlisle, and later Thomas Andrews. Though Titanic would become the most infamous of the trio, Olympic's construction began first, approximately three and a half months earlier than her sister. This scheduling decision was made for practical reasons, allowing the shipbuilders to refine techniques and ensure smooth progression for the subsequent vessels.

---

[33] https://sirwilliamarrol.wordpress.com/arrol-co-ltd/arrol-gantry/

Titanic (Left) and Olympic (Right) under construction. Library of
Congress, Washington, D.C. (file no. LC–USZ62–67359)

Aware of the public fascination with these grand ships, and
anticipating extensive media coverage during construction, the
White Star Line made a conscious decision to paint Olympic's
hull in white during her build. This choice served not only to
distinguish her visually from Titanic's later black hull, but also
to create a striking image in the many photographs expected
to circulate worldwide. Before her entry into active service,
however, Olympic would be repainted to match the traditional
White Star Line livery of a black hull with a gold stripe along
the upper deck.

Construction of Olympic followed the traditional shipbuilding process of the time: from the keel up. First came the

double-bottom—a vital feature designed to enhance the ship's structural integrity and safety—followed by the towering steel framework, then the immense hull plates, and finally the superstructure. Unlike modern vessels, which are typically welded, Olympic's hull was assembled from more than 2,000 steel plates fastened with millions of hand-driven rivets, many of which required teams of workers to heat, hammer, and seal each one individually. The sheer scale of the ship and the precision required to assemble her frame represented a monumental feat of Edwardian engineering. It would take approximately 26 months to complete Olympic's hull and superstructure—a process that would be echoed in the construction of Titanic, which remained a skeletal structure at the time of Olympic's launch.

On October 20th, 1910[34], Olympic was launched from her slipway into the waters of Belfast Lough. Contrary to popular depictions, including the dramatized film *A Night to Remember*, White Star Line maintained a longstanding policy of not christening its vessels with the ceremonial breaking of a bottle—a tradition they saw as unnecessary pageantry. Olympic was no exception, sliding down the greased slip in a spectacle of steel and steam, cheered on by thousands of spectators. Notably, White Star Line is said to have filmed the launch in early color—a rarity for the time—but unfortunately, this footage has not survived or been located to date.

After her launch, Olympic was towed to a fitting-out basin and then to dry dock, where her white construction hull was replaced with the standard black, and her four prominent orange-colored funnels were installed. This phase of construction

---

[34] https://www.britannica.com/topic/Olympic

also saw the completion of her lavish interiors and passenger accommodations, which would set new standards for luxury at sea. On May 29th, 1911, Olympic underwent her sea trials, which she passed with ease. Though no full speed tests were conducted at this time, the vessel proved herself seaworthy and stable, ready to claim her place as the largest ship in the world.

* * *

White Star Line made clever use of the publicity surrounding these events. Olympic's official departure from Belfast occurred on the same day as the launch of her sister ship Titanic, allowing both liners to share the spotlight and generate international interest. The synchronized events were accompanied by joint celebrations, a marketing strategy that underscored White Star's dominance in the transatlantic travel market.

Like her sister ships and all White Star vessels, Olympic was officially registered to the port city of Liverpool. However, in practice, she would rarely call there. Instead, Olympic was destined to operate out of the port of Southampton, which had become the company's new southern hub for its major Atlantic crossings. From Southampton, Olympic would begin her service to the world—a ship that would not only make history, but also outlive her more famous sister and remain in operation for nearly a quarter-century.

Olympic's construction marked a pivotal moment in maritime history. She embodied the height of Edwardian shipbuilding and heralded a new age of ocean travel—an age of grandeur,

THE OLYMPIAN'S

rivalry, and, for a time, unshakable optimism in the power of human engineering.

3

Chapter 3

Maiden voyage and Sister Lost

The maiden voyage of the R.M.S. *Olympic* was a landmark event in maritime history, signaling not only the debut of a new vessel but the dawn of a new standard in transatlantic travel. As the first of the *Olympic*-class ocean liners, she was the pride of the White Star Line and the physical embodiment of their ambition to dominate the North Atlantic shipping lanes. More than just a ship, *Olympic* was a floating palace—an engineering marvel whose very existence drew global attention.

On June 14, 1911, under much fanfare and public anticipation, *Olympic* departed Southampton on her maiden voyage. Her first stop was the port of Cherbourg, France, where she embarked additional passengers via specially designed tenders, *Nomadic* and *Traffic*, before continuing on to Queenstown (now Cobh), Ireland. From there, with a total of 1,313 passengers on board—many of them wealthy, notable, or influential—she set course for New York City across the vast Atlantic.[35]

Captain Edward Smith as in the New York Times, Courtesy Wiki Commons

[35] https://www.titanicandco.com/olympic/olympiccareer.html

Commanding *Olympic* for this momentous journey was Captain Edward Smith, one of White Star Line's most trusted and experienced officers. Smith had joined the company in 1880 as a fourth officer and steadily climbed the ranks, becoming a captain in 1887. His leadership of the *R.M.S. Majestic* during the Boer War—where he was tasked with transporting troops—earned him high praise and bolstered his reputation for composure and competence under pressure.[36]

Among the transatlantic elite, Captain Smith was known unofficially as "the millionaires' captain."[37] Affable, confident, and composed, he became the preferred choice of the wealthy and influential, many of whom requested voyages specifically under his command. It was therefore no surprise that when the White Star Line sought to launch its most ambitious liner yet, they turned to Smith to ensure the *Olympic's* maiden voyage was a resounding success.

The journey itself was smooth and uneventful—just as a maiden voyage should be. Passengers reveled in the unmatched luxury aboard the vessel, which featured grand dining saloons, lavish staterooms, and an atmosphere of stately opulence. The Atlantic proved kind, and *Olympic* made steady progress toward her destination.

However, upon her arrival in New York on June 21, 1911, the massive liner encountered a minor hiccup. While maneuvering into her berth with the assistance of tugboats, one of the smaller vessels became trapped beneath *Olympic's* enormous

---

[36] https://mollybrown.org/captain-smith/

[37] https://www.britannica.com/biography/Edward-J-Smith

stern. Although the tugboat was eventually freed with no major damage to either craft, the incident foreshadowed the issues that would follow *Olympic* throughout her service life. For Captain Smith, the event did little to dent his sterling reputation—but it hinted at the consequences of navigating ships of such unprecedented scale.

Far more serious trouble loomed just a few months later. On September 20, 1911, while departing Southampton harbor, the *Olympic* collided with the Royal Navy's armored cruiser, H.M.S. *Hawke*.[38] The *Hawke*, designed for ramming enemy vessels, struck *Olympic* on her starboard side near the stern, tearing a gaping 40-foot gash below the waterline. The impact damaged *Olympic's* starboard propeller shaft and several watertight compartments.

Thanks to the ship's advanced design—particularly its series of watertight compartments—flooding was contained, averting disaster. The *Hawke*, however, did not fare as well. Her bow, designed to withstand impact, was crushed and twisted, a testament to the sheer mass and resilience of *Olympic*.

---

[38] https://www.usni.org/magazines/proceedings/1911/december/collision-between-h-ms-hawke-and-r-m-s-olympic

The Hole in the "Olympic," the Damage Below the Waterline being Much Greater Than That Above

The Bow of the "Hawke," the Damage being so Great That the Ram Has Been Mashed Flat

Popular Mechanics Magazine, 1911; courtesy WikiCommons

The collision sparked immediate controversy. White Star Line and the Royal Navy each blamed the other. White Star argued that the *Hawke* had failed to observe proper signaling protocols and had encroached on *Olympic's* right of way. The Admiralty, in contrast, claimed the fault lay with the *Olympic* herself. According to their version of events, the massive liner displaced such a vast volume of water while underway that it generated a suction effect, drawing the *Hawke* inward and causing the collision.

The fact that *Olympic* suffered significant damage comes as no surprise, as the H.M.S *Hawke* was designed to ram and sink ships. She was meant to do what she did, though facing such a large vessel such of *Olympic* was not anticipated. In the aftermath, both ships limped back to port. The discussion of who exactly had caused the incident in question soon emerged, with White Star Line and the Royal Navy immediately began pointing fingers at each other.

White Star claimed that the *Hawke* had failed to yield the right of way or properly signal the *Olympic*. The Royal Navy, on the other hand, argued that the immense size of the *Olympic* caused such a displacement of water that it sucked the smaller *Hawke* toward her, leading to the collision.[39]

> "I saw the cruiser coming along the starboard bow then, a few minutes afterwards, I saw the cruiser coming up almost parallel too our course."
> ~First Officer Murdock; admiralty court hearing, 1911. [40]

This royal navy's argument—the hydrodynamic suction theory—would become a key point in the ensuing legal dispute. Though heavily debated, the Admiralty Court ultimately found the White Star Line liable for the incident, citing that *Olympic* had not maintained a safe course in such confined waters. The ruling would cast a shadow over *Olympic's* otherwise glamorous debut and delay her service for several weeks as repairs were undertaken

Though financially costly, the collision inadvertently contributed to the myth of the "unsinkable" ships. The fact that the *Olympic* remained afloat after such damage, coupled with

---

[39] https://www.scientificamerican.com/article/the-andldquohawkeandrdquo-andldquoo/

[40] http://www.williammurdoch.net/articles_29_to_the_bitter_end_09.html

her extensive watertight compartments, fueled the belief that the *Olympic*-class liners, including the R.M.S. *Titanic*, were practically indestructible. This perception would later haunt White Star Line when the *Titanic* met her tragic fate, with many viewing the disaster as the ultimate downfall of hubris.

Following the collision with H.M.S. *Hawke*, the *Olympic* underwent temporary repairs that enabled her to remain in service for a short period. However, the extent of the damage—particularly to her starboard side and propeller shaft—necessitated a full return to Harland & Wolff's shipyard in Belfast for comprehensive restoration. This unexpected development had a significant ripple effect. With resources limited and tight construction schedules in place, the repair of the *Olympic* took precedence over the ongoing assembly of her sister ship, the *Titanic*. Among the redirected materials was a new propeller shaft originally manufactured for the *Titanic*, which was reassigned to the *Olympic* to expedite her return to service.

The delay in completing the *Olympic*'s repairs slowed progress on the *Titanic*, pushing back her maiden voyage. After six weeks of intense labor, the *Olympic* returned to trans-Atlantic duty, though her streak of misfortunes was far from over.

On February 24, 1912, while making her return voyage from New York, the *Olympic* encountered yet another setback—this time, a blade from her port-side propeller broke off.[41] Though the ship was never in danger, she had to return once again to Belfast for repairs. This further disrupted the final

---

[41] https://www.jmilford-titanic.com/2013/11/olympic-loses-propeller-blade.html

preparations of the *Titanic*, whose own departure had already been postponed. Originally slated to sail on March 20, the *Titanic*'s maiden voyage was officially delayed to April 10, 1912, in order to accommodate the urgent repair needs of her older sister.[42]

Olympic at Harland & Wolff for propeller blade repairs

[42] https://historicaleventsblog.weebly.com/realtimehistoryblog/the-rms-ol ympic-delays-titanics-maiden-voyage

A persistent maritime rumor emerged from this period, suggesting that the *Olympic*'s replacement propeller blade came directly from the *Titanic* herself. While no conclusive evidence exists to confirm this, the possibility underscores just how intertwined the fates of these two legendary ships were during their early histories.

It was also during this chapter of shared repairs and adjustments that the only known photograph of the *Titanic* and *Olympic* together was taken. Captured at the Harland & Wolff shipyards, the image immortalized a rare and poignant moment—two of the largest, most ambitious ocean liners of their time side by side. Though they were designed to be trans-Atlantic running mates—departing opposite ends of the ocean in tandem—logistics and scheduling meant their paths would rarely physically intersect. Even in their heyday, such a scene was considered exceptional.

As April 1912 approached, preparations for the *Titanic*'s long-awaited maiden voyage intensified. Captain Edward J. Smith, who had commanded the *Olympic* on her inaugural journey and many subsequent crossings, was reassigned to helm the new flagship of the White Star Line. With his departure, command of the *Olympic* was handed over to Captain Herbert James Haddock, an experienced officer in his own right, though lacking the towering reputation of his predecessor. Captain Smith brought with him several of his trusted officers and crew from the *Olympic*, seeking familiarity and reliability aboard the brand-new vessel.

* * *

Unlike her celebrated maiden voyage in 1911, the *Olympic*'s subsequent crossings lacked the grandeur and enthusiasm that once surrounded her. The ship, once hailed as the pinnacle of modern maritime engineering, would now sail under the shadow of her newer, grander sister—the *Titanic*. There were no jubilant send-offs or grand receptions awaiting her in port. The fanfare had shifted entirely to *Titanic*, the White Star Line's latest and most luxurious addition, whose imminent maiden voyage captured the attention of the world press and the public alike.

As *Olympic* quietly continued her scheduled transatlantic service, slipping in and out of Southampton and New York with practiced regularity, the eyes of the world watched the *Titanic* prepare for her historic crossing. But the attention lavished upon her would soon become a haunting footnote in history—her name forever associated not with triumph, but with unprecedented tragedy.

On the night of April 14, 1912, *Olympic* was midway through her return voyage from New York to Southampton when distress signals from the *Titanic* began to crackle through the wireless. Captain Herbert James Haddock[43], commanding officer aboard the *Olympic*, quickly grasped the severity of the messages and ordered an immediate change of course. Despite being some 505 nautical miles away—far too distant to render timely aid—he ordered the ship to proceed at full speed toward *Titanic*'s last reported position, hoping for a miracle.[44]

They were not alone. Other ships in the area began racing toward the scene, but it was Cunard's RMS *Carpathia*, approxi-

---

[43] https://www.titanicofficers.com/titanic_12_haddock_04.html

[44] https://www.bbc.com/news/magazine-17631595

mately 58 miles from the disaster, that would ultimately arrive first. As *Olympic* surged through the night toward the icy North Atlantic, *Carpathia* transmitted a chilling message: the *Titanic* had gone down in the early hours of April 15. The great ship was lost, and with her, over 1,500 souls. Only 705 survivors had been rescued and were now aboard *Carpathia*, bound for New York.

Stricken by the news, *Olympic*'s crew and passengers were deeply shaken. Captain Haddock transmitted an offer to take on the survivors to ease *Carpathia*'s burden. But this proposal was declined by White Star Line Chairman J. Bruce Ismay— himself one of the *Titanic*'s surviving passengers. Ismay feared the survivors would be horrified to board a ship that so closely resembled the vessel they had just escaped, down to its identical interiors and towering superstructure.[45] In light of this, *Olympic* had no choice but to resume her course to Southampton, where she arrived on April 21 to a somber and subdued reception.

The aftermath of the *Titanic* disaster ignited immediate calls for maritime reform and exposed glaring inadequacies in safety regulations, even aboard the esteemed *Olympic*. Public confidence in ocean liners plummeted, and White Star Line found itself scrambling to address safety concerns. In a hasty response, the company sourced 40 collapsible lifeboats from decommissioned troopships and loaded them onto *Olympic*. But far from restoring order, the measure sparked turmoil among the crew.

A group of 284 stokers—the men who toiled deep in the

---

[45] https://www.encyclopedia-titanica.org/roaming-around-memoirs-marc oni-operator.html

ship's engine rooms shoveling coal into her massive furnaces—refused to sail.[46] They voiced fears that the collapsible lifeboats were unreliable and that, even with the additions, the ship still lacked adequate lifeboats for everyone aboard. Determined to keep *Olympic* on schedule, White Star Line attempted to hire 100 non-union laborers as temporary replacements. Instead of calming the waters, this decision stirred more unrest. Concerned about safety and the experience level of the new hires, more crew members walked off the vessel in protest.

Tensions escalated to the point where a bold, if somewhat desperate, suggestion emerged: that prominent passengers, including the Duke of Sutherland, might help man the ship at least until it reached Ireland, where more qualified crew could be taken aboard.[47] However, the idea was quickly abandoned, likely deemed impractical and emblematic of the chaos that had descended upon the once-proud liner.

Even the intervention of naval authorities failed to quell the dissent. Ultimately, several of the striking stokers were arrested and charged with mutiny. However, public sentiment leaned in their favor, and local courts declined to issue harsh sentences, recognizing the extraordinary nature of the situation and the crew's genuine fear for their lives.

Faced with mounting pressure and delayed departures, White Star Line was forced to cancel *Olympic*'s next scheduled voyage. In a more measured and permanent response, the company replaced the collapsible lifeboats with conventional wooden lifeboats and increased overall lifeboat capacity—steps that

---

[46] https://stories.workingclasshistory.com/article/9616/rms-olympic-strike

[47] https://www.titanicofficers.com/titanic_12_haddock_05.html

finally reassured the crew. Only after these changes did the stokers agree to return to work, and *Olympic* was once again cleared for service.

* * *

In the wake of Titanic's catastrophic sinking, both the United States and the United Kingdom launched formal investigations into the tragedy.[48] These high-profile inquiries aimed not only to determine the causes of the disaster but also to recommend critical changes to maritime safety protocols. As Titanic's nearly identical sister ship, *Olympic* played an unexpected yet vital role in these investigations. Her construction, layout, and handling characteristics made her an ideal stand-in for forensic testing. Engineers and investigators used *Olympic* to conduct a series of simulations to better understand what might have transpired aboard *Titanic* during her final harrowing hours. Among the scenarios tested was whether *Titanic* could have successfully maneuvered to avoid the iceberg altogether. The conclusion, though sobering, was clear: while evasive action might have been possible under perfect conditions, a combination of delayed reaction, limited visibility, and high speed rendered the collision almost inevitable.

By the autumn of 1912, with public trust in ocean liners badly shaken, White Star Line made the difficult but necessary decision to temporarily withdraw *Olympic* from service for an

---

[48] https://www.britannica.com/topic/Titanic/Aftermath-and-investigation

extensive refit at Harland & Wolff shipyards in Belfast.[49] While her sister ship *Britannic*—still under construction—would benefit from newly integrated safety designs, *Olympic* required retrofitting within the constraints of her existing architecture. This made the process more complicated and, in some cases, less efficient.

Instead of a wider double hull like the one being installed on *Britannic*, *Olympic* received a thick internal watertight skin running along the lower portion of her hull, a compromise that cost her some interior space but vastly increased her survivability. Her watertight bulkheads were extended higher, now reaching as far as B Deck, providing better compartmentalization in the event of hull breach. An additional bulkhead was also added, increasing the number of watertight compartments. However, not all advancements could be applied. *Olympic's* deck design could not accommodate the massive gantry davits designed to carry and launch multiple lifeboats simultaneously—an innovation *Britannic* would feature. Instead, *Olympic* retained the older Wellin davits, which limited the number of lifeboats she could carry at each station. To compensate, her boat deck was widened, and extra lifeboats were installed wherever space allowed.

Despite these technical limitations, *Olympic* emerged from her refit markedly safer. The upgrades meant she could likely survive the same hull damage that had doomed Titanic. Yet the illusion of invincibility was gone. No longer would White Star or any other line claim a ship to be "unsinkable"—the term had become a bitter symbol of hubris. Still, White Star Line wasted no time promoting *Olympic's* enhanced safety

---

[49] https://atlanticliners.com/white_star_home/olympic_home/

CHAPTER 3

features in advertisements and public statements, keen to restore confidence among an apprehensive public.

With her modifications complete, *Olympic* returned to passenger service in early 1913, resuming her transatlantic duties with quiet efficiency. The years that followed, particularly 1913 and the early months of 1914, were marked by routine sailings and a gradual return of public trust. Yet the calm was fleeting.

In June 1914, the assassination of Archduke Franz Ferdinand in Sarajevo sent political shock waves across Europe, setting into motion the events that would soon erupt into the First World War. As tensions escalated and alliances were tested, *Olympic's* days as a peaceful passenger liner were numbered. Before long, she would be called into service not as a luxury vessel, but as a troopship, tasked with carrying soldiers instead of socialites, and navigating war-torn seas rather than charted Atlantic routes.

4

Chapter 4

Olympic goes to war

As the summer of 1914 wore on, the ominous shadow of war began to spread across Europe, casting a pall over daily life. The assassination of Austrian Archduke Franz Ferdinand in Sarajevo by Serbian nationalists had set off a political chain reaction. What should have been a localized conflict soon escalated, drawn out by a web of military alliances and rising national tensions. Nation after nation joined the fray, transforming a regional crisis into what would become the First World War.

On the continent, the implications were stark and immediate. Civilians could see the writing on the wall, and many began making plans to flee while they still could. For some, escape was impossible—whether by conscription, political ties, or simply having nowhere to go. Others made desperate bids to reach neutral nations such as the Netherlands, Switzerland, or

Spain. But the largest wave of departures came from Americans, who, as citizens of a neutral power, sought to return home. This exodus brought a sudden, sharp increase in westbound bookings aboard British and French ocean liners. In this brief window—after war seemed inevitable but before Britain's entry—the transatlantic liners scrambled to accommodate the rush.

That window slammed shut on August 4, 1914, when the United Kingdom declared war on the German Empire after the latter ignored an ultimatum demanding the withdrawal of troops from neutral Belgium.[50] Britain was now a full participant in the growing conflict, and with that, the nature of ocean travel changed overnight. Crossing the Atlantic on British-flagged vessels became an exercise in peril.

By early 1915, the threat had intensified. Germany launched its policy of unrestricted submarine warfare, giving U-boats license to attack any ship—even neutral ones—deemed to be aiding the Allied war effort. The ocean, once a route of luxury and commerce, had become a hunting ground. One of the most harrowing demonstrations of this shift came on May 7, 1915, with the sinking of the RMS *Lusitania*. Over 1,100 lives were lost, including 128 Americans.[51] The tragedy shocked the world and served as a grim warning: no ship was truly safe.

Transatlantic passenger travel dropped sharply as a result. Immigration slowed to a trickle, and leisurely crossings became almost nonexistent. Shipping lines attempted to adapt: ships

---

[50] https://www.theguardian.com/world/2014/aug/05/england-declares-war-germany-1914

[51] https://www.loc.gov/collections/world-war-i-rotogravures/articles-and-essays/the-lusitania-disaster/

were rerouted to ports such as Liverpool or Glasgow, away from the more exposed Southampton. They were painted in wartime grays and began sailing under blackout conditions, extinguishing all lights to avoid detection by lurking submarines.[52]

Still, passenger numbers dwindled. The White Star Line, faced with financial and operational uncertainties, made the difficult decision to withdraw its flagship, RMS *Olympic*, from service. Her final commercial voyage departed New York in late October 1914 with only 153 passengers on board—an astonishingly low number for a ship designed to carry thousands.[53]

But *Olympic*'s last peacetime voyage would take an unexpected turn. On October 27, 1914, while crossing the Atlantic, the ship received distress signals from the British battleship HMS *Audacious*, which had struck a German mine off the Irish coast. The *Olympic* rushed to assist, successfully rescuing the majority of the crew. The event, however, became politically sensitive. The British Admiralty, fearing a blow to national morale, imposed a strict communications blackout. *Olympic* was ordered to Lough Swilly, Ireland, and detained there in secrecy.[54]

---

[52] http://titanic-cad-plans.website/wp-content/uploads/2023/06/Color-Guide-for-the-Olympic-Class-Ships.pdf

[53] https://oceanlinersmagazine.com/2020/10/27/olympic-races-sinking-battleship/

[54] https://www.titanicofficers.com/titanic_12_haddock_07.html

*Sinking of the H.M.S Audacious as seen from the deck of Olympic;
courtesy Wiki Commons*

Despite protests from prominent individuals—most notably American steel tycoon Charles Schwab, who had been aboard—the ship was not allowed to continue her journey until November 2. She then sailed to Belfast to disembark her remaining passengers, and it was expected that she would be laid up for the duration of the war. But destiny had other ideas.

In May 1915, the British Admiralty formally requisitioned *Olympic* for use as a troop transport.[55] At first, both White Star and naval authorities were hesitant. The Admiralty feared that *Olympic*'s sheer size made her an obvious and vulnerable target.

---

[55] https://www.britannica.com/topic/Olympic

Meanwhile, the company lamented the loss of its premier liner and the stripping of her lavish interiors. But war has little patience for sentiment. The need for large, fast transports outweighed these concerns.

Olympic was hastily converted. Her ornate fittings were removed, her grand staterooms gutted. Guns were mounted on deck, and accommodations were refitted to carry up to 6,000 troops. Renamed HMT (His Majesty's Transport) *Olympic*, she was thrust into an entirely new role: no longer a floating palace, but a workhorse of war.

Her first assignments took her to the eastern Mediterranean, ferrying troops to support the ill-fated Gallipoli campaign. From late 1915 through early 1916, *Olympic* made voyage after voyage, enduring long journeys and difficult conditions. When the campaign collapsed in failure, she was redirected to transatlantic routes, this time carrying Canadian troops to France via Britain.[56]

After the United States joined the war in April 1917, *Olympic* expanded her role yet again. American "doughboys" began boarding her decks, bound for the Western Front. It was during this period that the ship received a striking new look— *dazzle camouflage*, a chaotic paint pattern designed to confuse submarine rangefinders and make it harder to judge a ship's speed and heading. The liner became a familiar sight in military ports, earning the nickname "Old Reliable" from the soldiers who sailed aboard her.

---

[56] https://scholars.wlu.ca/cmh/vol11/iss1/6/

H.M.T Olympic in Dazzle Camouflage; courtesy
thedreamstress.com

Her reputation for dependability only grew after a dramatic encounter on May 12, 1918. While sailing westbound, *Olympic* spotted the German U-boat U-103 surfacing in preparation to fire. Acting quickly, her crew opened fire, and the ship turned to ram. With a shuddering blow, *Olympic*'s massive propellers tore into the submarine, crippling it and forcing its crew to abandon ship.[57] Though merchant vessels had been instructed to ram U-boats if possible, *Olympic* remains the only passenger liner known to have successfully done so. The survivors of U-103 were later picked up by the American destroyer USS *Davis*.

It wasn't *Olympic*'s first brush with disaster. In 1917, she had narrowly avoided destruction when another U-boat, U-53, fired a torpedo that struck her hull but failed to explode—a fact discovered only after the war, when damaged plates were inspected in dry dock.[58]

Over the course of the war, *Olympic* carried over 201,000 troops and steamed thousands of miles through hostile waters.[59] Her reliability, speed, and size made her an invaluable asset. She had gone from a symbol of prewar luxury to one of wartime resilience, and in doing so, secured her place in naval history.

By the time the armistice was signed in November 1918, *Olympic* had earned the deep respect of her crew, her passengers, and the public. She had weathered storms, mines, torpedoes, and the chaos of global conflict—and returned, steadfast and

---

[57] https://oceanlinersmagazine.com/2020/05/11/olympic-sinks-u-boat/

[58] https://travelswithanthony.wordpress.com/2013/10/28/rms-olympic-the-old-reliable-evaluated/

[59] https://www.thevintagenews.com/2016/11/25/in-wwi-the-rms-olympic-won-a-battle-with-a-u-boat/

proud, as "Old Reliable."

5

Chapter 5

Return to civilian life

In the immediate aftermath of World War I, R.M.S. *Olympic* remained under the control of the British Admiralty for several more months. This was hardly surprising; with the guns of Europe finally silent, millions of soldiers and support staff needed repatriation from the continent. Ocean liners, with their vast capacities and speed, became the ideal solution to this logistical challenge. *Olympic*, with her proven wartime record and reputation as "Old Reliable," was kept in service a little longer to help bring the troops home.

However, as the urgency of demobilization eased and peace-time normalcy began to take root, the need for military transport diminished. The *Olympic's* wartime dazzle camouflage—an angular, geometric pattern once meant to confuse German U-boats—was now obsolete. In early 1919, her striking paint scheme was hastily replaced with her prewar livery: a black hull, white superstructure, and buff-colored funnels. But the repainting was done in haste, resulting in a patchy, uneven appearance that bore little of the elegance she had once been known for.

By August 16, 1919, Olympic was formally released from military service and returned to her original owners, the White Star Line.[60] Eager to restore their flagship to her former glory, the company immediately sent her back to Harland & Wolff in Belfast for a comprehensive postwar refit. The ship had endured the rigors of war for nearly five years—her interiors gutted, her machinery pushed to the limits, and her structure subjected to constant strain. She now required more than just cosmetic attention.

Among the most significant upgrades was the conversion of her propulsion system. *Olympic's* coal-burning boilers, once tended by legions of stokers, were replaced or modified to burn oil fuel, a far more efficient and cleaner energy source.[61] This modernization dramatically reduced crew requirements and cut operating costs, while also increasing the ship's speed and reliability. At the same time, her grand public rooms—stripped bare during her wartime service—were meticulously restored or reimagined, blending Edwardian opulence with emerging modern design sensibilities of the 1920s.

When Olympic emerged from her extensive overhaul in June 1920, she was, in many ways, a rejuvenated ship. Though now nearly a decade old, she had been reborn with a new identity that balanced tradition with innovation. She resumed

---

[60] http://thegreatoceanliners.com/articles/olympic/

[61] https://markchirnside.co.uk/wp-content/uploads/2022/11/Olympic_suit es1929-1.pdf

passenger service across the North Atlantic the following month, greeted by an eager public nostalgic for the grandeur of prewar travel.

Yet the landscape of transatlantic shipping had changed profoundly. *Olympic* was now alone; her beloved sisters were gone. *Titanic*, tragically lost on her maiden voyage in 1912, and *Britannic*, converted to a hospital ship and sunk in the Aegean Sea during the war in 1916. Though designed as part of a triumphant trio, *Olympic* would never sail alongside her sister ships as once intended.

In the early 1920s, the White Star Line began rebuilding its fleet. Two notable acquisitions joined *Olympic* on the North Atlantic route. The first was the R.M.S. *Homeric*, originally built as the *Columbus* for the German Norddeutscher Lloyd line but ceded to Britain as part of Germany's war reparations.[62] The second, far grander addition was the R.M.S. *Majestic*, formerly the *SS Bismarck*, the largest passenger ship in the world at the time and originally constructed for the Hamburg–America Line.[63] Like *Homeric*, *Majestic* came into British hands through the provisions of the Treaty of Versailles, which redistributed much of the defeated Central Powers' maritime assets.

---

[62] https://www.whitestarhistory.com/homeric

[63] https://www.greatoceanliners.com/ss-bismarck-rms-majestic

WHITE STAR LINE

R.M.S. "OLYMPIC" (Triple Screw), 46,439 Tons.

— THE —

R.M.S. "MAJESTIC" 56,551 tons

THE LARGEST STEAMER IN THE WORLD
(RECORD TRIP FROM NEW YORK TO CHERBOURG)

R.M.S. "OLYMPIC" - 46,439 tons

R.M.S. "HOMERIC" - 34,356 tons

MAINTAIN AN EXPRESS
WEEKLY MAIL SERVICE

Between

Southampton - Cherbourg - New York

Advertisement of Service by Olympic, Majestic, and Homeric[64]

Together, this trio—*Olympic, Homeric*, and *Majestic*—formed the cornerstone of White Star's postwar operations. Though somewhat eclectic in design and origin, they each carried the prestige of international liners and helped restore the company's dominance on the Atlantic run. While *Olympic* never realized her creators' vision of sailing in formation with her original sisters, she found enduring success in this unexpected fleet. She became not just a link to the past but a vital presence in a world struggling to move forward.

* * *

With her conversion to an oil-burning vessel, *R.M.S. Olympic* entered a new era of efficiency and profitability. The modernization dramatically reduced the number of crew needed to maintain her propulsion systems—no longer did legions of firemen and trimmers toil in sweltering boiler rooms, shoveling coal day and night. Oil was not only cleaner and easier to manage, but it was also far more cost-effective. As a result, Olympic became one of the most economically viable ships in the White Star Line's fleet during the early 1920s.

Throughout the decade, Olympic remained a popular choice among transatlantic travelers, especially the wealthy and the well-connected. She exuded an old-world charm that her newer contemporaries lacked—a sense of grandeur and nostalgia that resonated deeply with those who remembered

---

[64] https://www.ggarchives.com/OceanTravel/ImmigrantShips/Olympic.html

the gilded age of prewar ocean travel. From celebrities and business magnates to politicians and socialites, many chose to sail aboard the venerable liner. For a time, *Olympic* was not just a ship—she was a living legend, a tangible link to a bygone era.

But *Olympic's* long-standing reputation for collisions—a trait that had earned her the unfortunate nickname "Old Reliable" for reasons both admiring and ironic—would come back to haunt her once again,

On May 22nd, 1924, while berthed in New York Harbor, Olympic was maneuvering when she collided with the Furness Bermuda Line's *Fort St. George*.[65] The incident appeared minor at first—only superficial damage was visible—but further inspection revealed a far more serious situation. The structural frame of her stern had been compromised. Though the immediate consequences were downplayed in the press, it became clear that Olympic would need to return to Harland & Wolff in Belfast for significant repairs.

Once in dry dock, engineers discovered the damage was far more extensive than initially believed. The entire stern frame of the ship needed to be replaced—a daunting challenge that had never before been undertaken on a vessel of her size and complexity. The operation would test the limits of contemporary shipbuilding and repair technology.

Despite the cost and complexity of the project, White Star Line remained committed to their flagship. They believed *Olympic* still had years of service left in her. Over the course of eight intensive weeks, skilled workers labored to complete the repairs, successfully installing a brand-new stern frame and

---

[65] https://www.nytimes.com/1924/03/23/archives/olympic-hits-liner-in-ri ver-3-injured-6-women-faint-as-huge.html

restoring the vessel to seaworthiness. It was a remarkable feat, further cementing *Olympic's* legacy as a ship that could endure and overcome nearly any obstacle.

And sail again she did.

The years that followed were among *Olympic's* most successful. She continued to cross the Atlantic with grace and reliability, earning the loyalty of repeat passengers and newcomers alike. Her interiors, a blend of Edwardian splendor and postwar refurbishment, still evoked awe. For a while, it seemed that *Olympic* had truly transcended her troubled past.

But this golden period was not to last.

With the advent of the great depression, *Olympic* and White Star Line would soon face a new challenge. One that can not easily be over come – Economics.

6

Chapter 6

Cunard-White Star Line

This chapter is not solely a continuation of *Olympic*'s story—it is a necessary detour into the fate of her parent company, the White Star Line. For one cannot fully understand the later years of *Olympic* without grasping the shifting tides that engulfed the company that created her. As the fortunes of the White Star Line rose and fell, so too did the course of its most enduring vessel. In truth, the histories of *Olympic* and White Star are entwined like strands of rope—separate, yet inseparable.

The first major turning point for White Star Line after the *Titanic* tragedy came not in policy or finances, but in the loss of leadership. J. Bruce Ismay, president of the International Mercantile Marine Company (IMM) and chairman of White Star, had been aboard *Titanic* during her fateful maiden voyage in April 1912. He survived the sinking—but in doing so, paid a price that no court could assign.

In the immediate aftermath, Ismay became the focus of public fury and media condemnation. Newspapers painted him as a coward and opportunist, a man of privilege who had supposedly taken a lifeboat seat from a woman or child. Whispers turned to rumors, and rumors to slander. Some claimed he had disguised himself as a woman to escape. Others, far more damaging, insisted he had pressured Captain Edward Smith to maintain high speed through iceberg-laden waters in a bid to break records and generate publicity for White Star.

None of these claims were ever substantiated. In both the British Board of Trade Inquiry and the U.S. Senate hearings, Ismay was ultimately exonerated. Testimonies showed that he had assisted in the evacuation, helping passengers into lifeboats before himself taking an empty seat in collapsible lifeboat C, well after many boats had already departed. Yet the damage to his reputation had already been done. The court of public opinion had found him guilty, and no official ruling could unring that bell.

Ismay, fully aware of the irreparable harm to his image, made no attempt to restore it. Instead, he quietly accepted the role of scapegoat. By 1913, after concluding the complicated process of handling Titanic's insurance settlements, Ismay resigned from both IMM and the White Star Line, vanishing from the helm of the very company he had once driven to prominence.

In the years that followed, Ismay withdrew from public life entirely, retreating to a private existence in relative obscurity. He refused to speak of the disaster, even to close family. Only shortly before his death, when his young grandson innocently asked if he had ever been in a shipwreck, did Ismay briefly acknowledge his past:

"Yes, I was once in a ship which was believed to be
unsinkable"
~ J. Bruce Ismay, 1936[66]

His granddaughter and biographer, Pauline Mataras, later
wrote that he never emotionally recovered from the events
of 1912. In her words, J. Bruce Ismay became "a corpse of his
former self", a man haunted not only by the ghosts of the North
Atlantic, but by the bitter realization that the world had cast
him as a villain in a tragedy where he had tried, in truth, to help.

Ismay died in 1937, in quiet seclusion, still burdened by the
shadow of *Titanic*.

* * *

With the resignation of J. Bruce Ismay in 1913, the White Star
Line entered a new era—one shaped less by vision and more
by survival. Leadership of the International Mercantile Marine
Company (IMM) fell first to Harold Sanderson, and later to
Philip Albright Small Franklin, both of whom faced a company
struggling to remain afloat in a rapidly shifting maritime world.
For White Star Line, these years were marked by slow decline, a
loss of identity, and eventual absorption into the hands of new
and uncertain leadership.

By the mid-1920s, IMM was in a dire financial state. Once

---

[66] Andrew (2012). Shadow of the Titanic: the extraordinary stories of those
who survived. Atria Books. ISBN 978-1451671568

envisioned as a global shipping trust that could rival all others, the company had become bloated, unprofitable, and burdened by outdated infrastructure and stiffening competition. Facing growing economic nationalism and increasing isolationist sentiment in the United States, IMM began exploring the option of divesting its British subsidiaries, including White Star. American lawmakers were also proposing shipping legislation that offered lucrative subsidies to U.S.-based operators—benefits IMM could not access so long as it held significant foreign interests.[67] It became not just prudent, but imperative, to cut the company loose.

At the same time, immigration restrictions in the United States, particularly the Immigration Act of 1924, dealt a severe blow to transatlantic passenger travel. With fewer immigrants crossing the ocean, demand for steerage and third-class tickets—once the bread and butter of lines like White Star—plummeted. The company's financial foundation was crumbling.

Into this precarious landscape stepped Sir Owen Philipps, known by his peerage title Lord Kylsant, head of the Belfast-based shipbuilding firm Harland & Wolff. For Philipps, the acquisition of the White Star Line in 1927[68] was not just a business transaction—it was the fulfillment of a personal dream. A man obsessed with building a global shipping empire, Philipps had begun his career in 1888 by founding his first maritime company. Over the years, he had aggressively expanded, acquiring ships and companies in pursuit of dominance on the

---

[67] https://titanichistoricalsociety.org/international-mercantile-marine-company/

[68] https://www.bandcstaffregister.com/page5604.html

high seas. White Star, for him, was the jewel in the crown.

Sir Owen Philipps; Courtesy of Wiki Commons

But what seemed like a crowning achievement would instead mark the beginning of a disastrous downfall.

In purchasing White Star Line, Lord Kylsant overextended himself financially, acquiring a company at a time when its resources were depleted by war and its balance sheets burdened with debts—especially substantial Treasury loans owed to the British government for wartime losses and expenditures. Nevertheless, he pressed forward with an ambitious plan to reorganize the Royal Mail Steam Packet Company (RMSPC)—his main holding—around White Star, attempting to center the new conglomerate's operations in Southampton, and focusing heavily on routes to Australia, where demand for passage was briefly booming.

Unfortunately, Lord Kylsant's timing could not have been worse.

To solidify this vision, he poured capital into acquiring additional shares in smaller shipping lines, hoping to dominate multiple routes and create economies of scale. However, the over expansion exposed the entire operation to market volatility. The gamble on Australian routes, in particular, backfired spectacularly. Over saturation of the route led to a rapid collapse in profitability, and White Star, now over-leveraged and over-committed, began to buckle under the weight of poor investments and mounting losses.

Then came the final, crushing blow—the Great Depression.

With global markets in free-fall and international trade grinding to a halt, the maritime industry suffered an unprecedented collapse. Rather than cut losses or downsize, Lord Kylsant attempted to keep the illusion of success alive. To maintain investor confidence, he secretly shuffled funds between divisions, propping up failing branches of the Royal Mail Group using money from the more stable ones.[69] For a time, this financial sleight of hand created the appearance of

[69] https://moneyweek.com/518105/great-frauds-in-history-lord-kylsant-and-rmspc

solvency, but it was built on deception.

In 1931, the truth came out. A government audit uncovered the scheme, and Lord Kylsant was arrested and charged with corporate fraud. At his trial, he pleaded his case, and tried to come up with various excuses for what he did.

> "We never tell shareholders how the balance of profit and loss is made up. . . . It is not easy for the average man to understand."
> ~ Lord Kylsant, July 1931[70]

In a scandal that rocked the British shipping world, he was convicted and imprisoned, becoming one of the few members of the British aristocracy to serve time for white-collar crime, though the sentence was for a total of 12 months. His dream of becoming the world's foremost shipping magnate had ended not with a triumph—but in disgrace.

The White Star Line, now deeply entangled in the wreckage of Lord Kylsant's failed empire, was a shadow of its former self. Its legacy ships—*Olympic* among them—remained symbols of a grander age, but the company that built them had lost its course.

* * *

---

[70] https://time.com/archive/6819282/great-britain-crown-v-kylsant/

As the 1920s waned, so too did the fortunes of RMS *Olympic*, once the pride of the White Star Line. In the wake of sweeping changes to U.S. immigration policy—most notably the Immigration Act of 1924—the once-thriving stream of third-class passengers crossing the Atlantic began to dry up.[71] For a company like White Star, which had long relied on immigrant traffic to fill the lower decks of its ocean liners, this marked a seismic shift.

To adapt, White Star made the decision to reconfigure *Olympic's* accommodations, introducing a more flexible "tourist class" aimed at attracting middle-class travelers. This new class, positioned between the luxury of first class and the austerity of steerage, was designed to appeal to a changing customer base—one increasingly comprised of tourists rather than emigrants. *Olympic* underwent a series of annual refits, each one relatively minor, but each signaling the ship's gradual evolution from a grand liner of the Edwardian era to a vessel struggling to remain relevant in the modern age.

Despite these efforts, 1929 would prove to be the last true peak of Olympic's illustrious career.

The onset of the Great Depression delivered a staggering blow to the transatlantic shipping industry. Passenger numbers plummeted, and shipping lines scrambled to find alternative sources of income. In response, White Star began to experiment with seasonal pleasure cruises[72], sending *Olympic* on summer voyages between New York and Halifax, a far cry from her

---

[71] https://web.archive.org/web/20160413123227/http://www.thegreatoceanliners.com/olympic.html

[72] https://www.countypress.co.uk/news/19642051.white-star-line-great-depression-booze-cruise-uplift/

former prestige. These cruises offered short escapes for those who could still afford travel, but they brought in only a fraction of the revenue that traditional Atlantic crossings once had.

During the winter months, when demand for ocean travel was marginally higher, White Star entered into a quiet cooperation with its old rival, Cunard.[73] In a rare show of pragmatism, the two companies began coordinating their sailing schedules, staggering departures to avoid direct competition on the same routes. It was a sign of desperation more than unity—two faltering giants trying to conserve dwindling resources.

By 1933, it became undeniable: *Olympic* was no longer profitable. Her maintenance costs were growing, and her aging infrastructure—still rooted in pre-war design—could no longer compete with the sleek, modern liners coming into service. White Star itself was nearing collapse, its financial situation growing more precarious with each passing month.

Then came May 10, 1934.

Under immense pressure from the British government, and with both companies teetering on the edge of insolvency, Cunard and White Star merged, forming the Cunard-White Star Line.[74] This consolidation was not born out of mutual admiration but out of necessity—primarily to secure government funding to complete Cunard's halted construction of the massive new liner that would eventually become the RMS *Queen Mary*.

The merger was a lifeline, but not for everyone. There was

---

[73] https://oceanlinersmagazine.com/2020/05/25/great-depression-creates-cruise-glut/

[74] https://manchesterhistorian.com/2015/cunard-a-voyage-through-history/

no sentimental consideration given to the older ships in either fleet. *Olympic*, once hailed as the "Old Reliable" for her sturdy service during peace and war, was now simply an aging asset, increasingly viewed as an obsolete burden.

As if to underscore her fading glory, just days after the merger, *Olympic* suffered the worst collision of her career—excluding her deliberate ramming and sinking of the German submarine *U-103* during the war. This latest accident further tarnished her already slipping reputation and sealed her fate in the eyes of Cunard-White Star management.

There would be no revival, no grand farewell tour for the once-mighty liner. Olympic had served faithfully for over two decades, weathered wars, collisions, and corporate collapse. But in the cold calculations of profit and progress, there was no longer room for sentiment.

Chapter 7

The Lightship

On the morning of May 14th, 1934, the RMS *Olympic*—once the majestic queen of the seas—was approaching New York Harbor, making her way through the dense waters off the coast of Nantucket. A thick wall of fog blanketed the sea, reducing visibility to a mere 500 feet. Despite her experience and age, *Olympic* was still a formidable vessel, but even the most seasoned of ships were no match for the treacherous waters and poor visibility off Nantucket.

Olympic, like many vessels navigating blind in such conditions, was homing in on a radio beacon from a nearby lightship—specifically, the Nantucket Lightship *LV-117*. Lightships, floating lighthouses anchored in perilous maritime zones, served a vital role in guiding ships safely along their paths.[75] In places like Nantucket Shoals, where constructing a traditional lighthouse was impossible, these vessels stood guard in the fog and storms, broadcasting either visual signals or, increasingly in the 20th century, radio pulses.

On board the *LV-117*, tension filled the air. The crew, small but dedicated, had reason to be on edge. Only months earlier, the lightship had been grazed by the SS *Washington*[76], a liner of the company United States Lines. That incident, though causing only minor damage, had rattled the men deeply—a chilling reminder of the vulnerability of their station, and their own fragile place in the vast, unforgiving sea.

LV-117 in 1931 per USCG via Wiki Commons

Still, the crew understood the risks. This was a dangerous post,

[75] https://www.marineinsight.com/types-of-ships/what-is-a-lightship/

[76] https://www.nelights.com/blog/the-nantucket-lightship-collision-with-the-rms-olympic/#gsc.tab=0

one of the most perilous on the East Coast. According to the official website of the *LV-112*, the lightship that would eventually replace *LV-117*, these waters were notoriously hazardous. Currents were unpredictable, fog was frequent, and the steady parade of ships—some of the largest in the world—passed within dangerously close range, often guided only by sound and blind luck.

> Lightship duty for crew members was extremely hazardous, especially on the Nantucket Shoals station — considered the most dangerous lightship assignment in the USCG and the world.[77]

Despite knowing full well the immense dangers of their post, nothing could have prepared the crew of Nantucket Lightship LV-117 for the sheer terror that unfolded on the morning of May 14, 1934. Imagine it: standing on the deck, shrouded in thick, choking fog, when suddenly—like a ghost from another world—the vast silhouette of the RMS Olympic loomed into view, bearing down directly upon them.

The lightship's crew would have had only seconds to react. Olympic, once the pride of the White Star Line, was a true behemoth—over 75 times the size and weight of the fragile lightship. Her mass and momentum were impossible to halt in the scant moments after the lightship was spotted. Similarly, LV-117 had no chance of evasive action. The distance was simply too small. Both crews, powerless to alter the inevitable,

---

[77] https://www.nantucketlightshiplv-112.org/lv-112.htm

could only stand frozen, watching helplessly as the collision bore down.

> *"I was looking out when I saw the Olympic coming. I could see the helmsman on her, putting his helm to starboard. I waved frantically at him to put her to port. If he had, he would have missed us. He evidently did not see or misunderstood my signals. The next thing I knew she struck us."*
> ~ *Captain George Braithwaite, LV-117*[78]

When Olympic struck, her massive hull smashed into the midsection of the lightship with devastating force. LV-117 stood no chance.[79] The overwhelming difference in mass and inertia crushed the smaller vessel instantly, tearing her apart like a toy. Those lightship crewmen who happened to be below decks at the moment of impact were likely killed instantly in the impact, trapped as the walls around them crumpled and the sea rushed in.

LV-117 sank in moments. The frigid Atlantic waters swallowed her wreckage, leaving only oil, wood, and bodies bobbing in the rolling waves.

To the credit of *Olympic's* officers and crew, once the ship had come to a halt, they acted quickly and decisively to render aid. Three of *Olympic's* lifeboats were lowered into the chilly waters. The rescuers worked desperately, combing through the debris and pulling survivors from the water. Of the lightship's

---

[78] https://www.lighthousedigest.com/Digest/StoryPage.cfm?StoryKey=4472

[79] https://eganmaritime.org/news/sinking-of-the-lv117

eleven-man crew, seven were recovered alive. Tragically, three of those seven would later succumb to their injuries, despite all efforts to save them.

Once the survivors were brought aboard and made as comfortable as possible, *Olympic* resumed her course, continuing on toward New York—but the terrible weight of the collision traveled with her, as did the knowledge that another tragedy now stained her long service record.

The four surviving Crew members of LV–117 rescued by the Olympic; Image: Photos, Inc via Lighthouse Digest

In the aftermath of the sinking, an investigation was launched, and the *Olympic* was ultimately found to be at fault. As a result, Cunard-White Star Line, the newly formed company overseeing *Olympic's* operations, was ordered to pay $500,000[80] in damages—an enormous sum at the time. These funds went toward the construction of a replacement lightship, LV-112, which was built with new safety features, including reinforced hull plating and updated technology, designed to make her as "indestructible" as possible.

LV-112 would go on to serve with distinction, guarding the Nantucket shoals for decades. In recognition of her service and the lives lost in her predecessor's tragic sinking, LV-112 was declared a National Historic Landmark in 1989. She remains afloat to this day, lovingly preserved and now moored in Boston as a living memorial to those who served aboard the lightships.

As for *Olympic*, the ship herself bore surprisingly little damage from the collision. Upon her return to Southampton, she was immediately dry-docked for inspection. Surveyors found only minor hull dents and crumpled plating—a testament to her rugged construction, but also a sobering reminder of how little a ship of her size was affected by destroying something so much smaller.

Yet the physical scars were not the only wounds *Olympic* carried. Financially, the great liner was already ailing, and the legal and public relations fallout from the Nantucket disaster only deepened her troubles. Passenger numbers were down, the costs of maintaining an aging ship were soaring, and the world she had once ruled was rapidly slipping away.

---

[80] https://acrobat.adobe.com/id/urn:aaid:sc:US:793ea9d3-87fa-413d-abc3-06141c47d587

8

Chapter 8

Scraping & Legacy

By 1935, time had finally caught up with the R.M.S. Olympic. Once the proud "Old Reliable" of the White Star Line, she had been sailing the North Atlantic for nearly a quarter of a century. But despite her legendary reputation and her loyal following, the aging liner had become a financial burden. For the past two years, Olympic had been operating at a loss, and with every passing month, it became clearer that she was no longer economically viable in a rapidly modernizing world.

The broader shipping industry was also in turmoil. The Great Depression had devastated global trade, slashed passenger numbers, and left many major lines scrambling for survival. To stay afloat, White Star Line, long a symbol of British maritime prestige, was forced into a merger with its fierce rival, the Cunard Line, forming the new Cunard-White Star Line. This consolidation was seen as a lifeline—but it came with consequences.

As the new company worked to stabilize its footing, it looked for ways to cut costs and eliminate redundancy. Unfortunately for Olympic, she was now seen as just that: redundant.

Before the merger, Cunard had already begun building a pair of revolutionary new ocean liners—the *Queen Mary* and *Queen Elizabeth*. These vessels were larger, faster, and fitted with the latest in luxury and safety innovations. Together, they were poised to dominate the transatlantic route between Southampton and New York, rendering older ships like *Olympic* obsolete. In the eyes of the new administration, there was no longer a place for her in the fleet.

In April 1935, after 24 years of service, the decision was made. *Olympic* was officially withdrawn from service and laid up in Southampton, stripped of her glory, awaiting her fate. Soon, she was put up for sale.

There was no shortage of interest. Some saw an opportunity to turn the iconic liner into a floating hotel or museum ship, with proposals floated for docking her off the coast of France or converting her into a luxurious static attraction. Even then, there were voices who recognized Olympic's historical value— as the last surviving sister of the Titanic, as a veteran of World War I, and as a beloved passenger liner who had carried more than 430,000 people across the Atlantic during her career.

But economic hardship spoke louder than sentiment. In the end, preservation lost out to practicality.

Olympic was sold for £97,500, equivalent to over £5.8 million in modern money as of 2025 - to Sir John Jarvis, a member of Parliament and philanthropist.[81] His goal wasn't to preserve

---

[81] https://youtu.be/qQkSUtO7Eb4?si=uTVpf_Wp79cNvBCb

the ship, but to use her dismantling as a form of economic relief.[82] The town of Jarrow, located in the northeast of England, had been ravaged by the Depression. Unemployment was widespread, and morale was at an all-time low. Sir Jarvis hoped that breaking Olympic apart would provide much-needed jobs to the struggling community.

[82] https://www.chroniclelive.co.uk/news/history/titanics-anniversary-reca ll-how-sister-11185220

Sir John Jarvis[83]

---

[83] https://www.southtyneside.gov.uk/article/20094/Sir-John-Jarvis-Given-Blue-Plaque-Tribute

And so, Olympic's long farewell began.

Over the next two years, the great ship was systematically stripped down. Her interior fittings—elegant wood paneling, ornate chandeliers, carved staircases, and fine brass work— were auctioned off, scattered across the country and around the world. Some found their way into hotels, movie theaters, and private homes. A few pieces, like the First-Class lounge panels and parts of her grand staircase, were preserved in unexpected places, even being incorporated into a hotel in Alnwick, Northumberland.

After the fittings were gone, the superstructure came next. Bit by bit, Olympic was reduced to a ghost of her former self. By late 1937, what remained of her hull was towed to Inverkeithing, Scotland, where the final act of her dismantling took place. By the end of that year, the last remnants of Olympic were gone— cut apart, melted down, and consigned to history.

Olympic's hull under tow for final scrapping[84]

For the people of Jarrow, Olympic's scrapping did provide a temporary economic boost and helped ease some of the town's suffering. But for maritime historians and enthusiasts, the decision to dismantle such a historic vessel remained a bitter pill to swallow.

Was it worth it to scrap a ship that had sailed for only 24 years, especially one of Olympic's pedigree and legacy?

At the time, some believed it was a short-sighted move:

> "I could understand the necessity if the 'Old Lady' had lost her efficiency, but the engines are as sound as they ever were."
>
> ~ Olympic Chief Engineer, 1935[85]

However, when reflecting on the past, it is all too easy to fall into the trap of retrospective thinking—viewing history through the lens of modern values and conveniences. Today, in an age where historical preservation is often prioritized, it seems almost unthinkable that a ship as storied and significant as the R.M.S. Olympic could be lost. But to truly understand the decisions made in the mid-1930s, we must set aside our contemporary perspective and step into the world as it existed then.

It has already been noted that both White Star Line and Cunard were in dire financial straits during this period. The

---

[84] http://rms-titanic.fr/otb/index/index_demolition.html

[85] https://www.forbes.com/sites/berniecarlson/2019/01/01/the-titanics-forgotten-sister/#393849af2706

Great Depression had brought the shipping industry to its knees. Passenger numbers were plummeting, operating costs remained high, and the once-thriving transatlantic trade was becoming increasingly unsustainable for aging vessels. For those living through that time, every penny counted, and survival—not sentiment—was the guiding principle.

Olympic was not the only casualty. Her longtime rival and contemporary, the R.M.S. *Mauretania*, a Cunard vessel built to compete with Olympic, met the breakers around the same time. The new Cunard-White Star merger was an act of consolidation, and with consolidation came hard decisions. Older vessels, no matter how beloved or historically significant, were liabilities on the balance sheet. The merged company was betting its future on newer, more efficient liners like the *Queen Mary*, which promised modern amenities, superior performance, and economic viability.

By 1935, *Olympic* was becoming increasingly difficult and expensive to maintain. She required almost annual refits, just to remain competitive with newer ships entering service. Her once state-of-the-art interiors had begun to feel outdated, her machinery worn, and her performance slipping. Despite her relatively young age by today's standards—just 24 years—she was older than many of her peers and suffered from a long history of accidents and incidents at sea.

When viewed through the cold logic of economics, the choice becomes clear. Olympic was unprofitable, aging, and demanding in upkeep. It is little surprise, then, that *when* the company needed to cut costs, *Olympic* was among the first to go. Once the decision was made to decommission her, her fate came down to a matter of simple arithmetic—who would buy her, and for what price.

And so, the curtain closed on the once-great R.M.S. *Olympic*. Her end came not with a grand farewell or commemorative voyage, but quietly, piece by piece, until she was no more. Yet, though the ship itself has long since vanished from the oceans she once ruled, her legacy endures.

For a time, some of *Olympic's* furnishings found a second life aboard the *Celebrity Millennium*, installed in a dining room meant to evoke the grandeur of ocean travel's golden age. Though these fittings were eventually removed during later refits, other artifacts survive. Fragments of *Olympic's* interior— the woodwork, lighting fixtures, paneling—can still be found in hotels, pubs, and private collections across the United Kingdom. Her ship's bell, a solemn artifact of maritime history, is preserved at the Titanic Historical Society in Springfield, Massachusetts.

Despite being frequently referred to as the "forgotten sister" of the *Titanic*, *Olympic* carved a path all her own. She enjoyed a successful, record-breaking peacetime career, played a vital role as a troopship during World War I, and safely transported hundreds of thousands of passengers across the Atlantic. Where *Titanic* tragically failed to complete even a single voyage, *Olympic* succeeded again and again. Her story is one of endurance, service, and reliability, and she deserves to be remembered as more than just a footnote to a disaster.

Perhaps, in another timeline, it was *Olympic* who captured the world's imagination, while Titanic faded quietly into obscurity. But history unfolded differently—and rightly so, *Titanic* has her own place in the world's collective memory.

Still, that should not diminish *Olympic's* place in history. She was the ship that proved what her sister never could: that the dream of the *Olympic*-class liners could endure. That grandeur, strength, and elegance could coexist. That legacy could be built not just on tragedy, but on a lifetime of service.

Let *Olympic* not be forgotten. Let her be honored, as she rightly should, for everything she was—and everything she achieved.

Chapter 9

A Legend Is Born

Wednesday, May 31, 1911 marked a momentous occasion at the Harland and Wolff Shipyard in Belfast, Ireland. After three years of meticulous design and labor-intensive construction, the RMS *Titanic*—hailed as the crown jewel of the White Star Line—was ready to take her first step toward immortality. This colossal vessel, envisioned to redefine the standard of oceanic travel, was structurally complete and poised to begin her journey toward outfitting and sea trials. At the time of her launch, Titanic assumed the title of the largest ship in the world from her sister ship, RMS *Olympic*, a testament to the relentless ambition of the White Star Line to outclass its rivals in both scale and luxury.

Though sisters in design, *Titanic* featured several subtle yet notable improvements over *Olympic*. These included more efficient piping systems, an enclosed forward promenade for added passenger comfort, and upgraded dining options that reflected the growing sophistication of transatlantic travel. Among these enhancements were an expanded À la Carte restaurant and the entirely new Café Parisien, which offered passengers an intimate slice of continental elegance at sea.

Nearly 100,000[86] spectators lined the shores of the River Lagan, watching in awe as Titanic majestically slid down the slipway, her massive hull meeting the water for the very first time. Despite maritime tradition, she was not christened with the ceremonial breaking of a bottle—an omission typical of White Star Line launches. Regardless, the launch was a spectacle, signaling the dawn of a new era in luxury ocean liners.

With her maiden voyage tentatively scheduled for March 20, 1912—coinciding with the first day of spring—Titanic's final outfitting commenced. Yet, fate intervened in a way that would alter maritime history forever. In September 1911, while Olympic was preparing for her fifth voyage from Southampton, disaster struck. The ship collided with the British warship HMS *Hawke*, sustaining significant damage to her hull. The collision necessitated extensive repairs, forcing Olympic to return to Belfast and drawing resources—both manpower and materials—away from Titanic's outfitting schedule. As a result, Titanic's maiden voyage was delayed by three weeks and rescheduled for April 10, 1912.[87]

Following Olympic's repairs, the urgency to complete Titanic intensified. The shipyard at Harland and Wolff became a hive of

---

[86] http://www.titanicandco.com/olympic.html

[87] https://historicaleventsblog.weebly.com/realtimehistoryblog/the-rms-olympic-delays-titanics-maiden-voyage

activity as workers redoubled their efforts. Every detail, from the grand staircase to the marbled Turkish baths, was finished with uncompromising precision, reflecting White Star Line's vision of a floating palace. The pride of Belfast was nearing her final form.

Yet another disruption arose in March 1912 when Olympic, back in service, returned to Belfast due to additional mechanical issues—this time the loss of one of her propeller blades.[88] Though a setback, the issue was resolved swiftly and did not derail Titanic's completion. In a rare and fleeting moment, both Olympic and Titanic stood side-by-side once more, this time as finished vessels—an awe-inspiring sight that captured the magnitude of the White Star Line's ambitions. Photographs of this encounter, now historical treasures, fueled decades of fascination and even conspiracies.

---

[88] https://atlanticliners.com/white_star_home/titanic_home/titanic-faq s-the-propeller-blade-mysteries/

Olympic (Left) and Titanic (Right) together in Belfast[89]

Some fringe theorists later claimed that the two ships were secretly switched, suggesting *Titanic* was actually *Olympic* under a different name—a theory unsupported by any credible evidence but one that continues to linger in popular lore, stoked by blurry photographs and the enduring mystery of *Titanic's* fate.

Regardless of such distractions, the focus remained firmly on *Titanic's* readiness. She was now the most opulent and advanced ship afloat, embodying human ingenuity and maritime engineering at its peak. On April 2, 1912, Titanic embarked on her sea trials in Belfast Lough with a skeleton crew

---

[89] https://commons.wikimedia.org/wiki/File:Olympic_and_Titanic_(cropped).jpg

aboard. These trials tested her speed, maneuverability, and emergency response capabilities. *Titanic* passed with flying colors, successfully demonstrating her stopping distances, turning circle, and maximum velocity. That same day, she was issued her "Agreement and Account of Voyages and Crew," a formal declaration of seaworthiness, valid for one year.

The ship then made her way to Southampton, eight days ahead of her now-scheduled maiden voyage. *Titanic* was more than just a ship—she was a symbol of a confident new century, a floating city designed not just to transport, but to inspire awe. Public perception, influenced by media reports, White Star's own marketing to a degree, and the sheer scale of the Olympic-class ships, began to embrace the notion that these vessels were practically unsinkable. Although the company technically never explicitly claimed it outright in any official capacity, the myth took root in the public imagination. Top brass at White Star Line were more than happy to egg on this statement.

> There is no danger that Titanic will sink. The boat is unsinkable and nothing but inconvenience will be suffered by the passengers."
> ~ Phillip Franklin, IMM vice-president, 1912[90]

* * *

---

[90] http://www.bbc.com/future/story/20120402-the-myth-of-the-unsinkable-ship

As the first blush of dawn unfurled across the Southampton skyline on the morning of April 10, 1912, a hushed awe settled over the White Star Line Pier. A soft golden hue shimmered across the calm waters, casting long reflections of the colossal RMS Titanic, moored proudly at the dock like a slumbering leviathan. Towering above the crowd, her four mighty funnels stood as symbols of industrial might and boundless ambition. The air crackled with anticipation, as men, women, and children from every walk of life gathered to witness history in motion—the departure of the world's most opulent ocean liner on her maiden voyage to the bustling shores of New York City.

This moment was more than just a departure; it was a celebration of a new era—one where engineering excellence met the gilded dreams of an increasingly connected world. Titanic, the crowning jewel of the White Star Line, was the physical embodiment of modernity, adorned in polished oak, gleaming brass, and the finest luxuries available to humankind. With every rivet, she whispered of progress and prestige, capturing the imagination of a generation determined to chase the horizon.

The process of boarding this floating palace mirrored the rigid social divisions that defined Edwardian society. First-Class passengers—an illustrious collection of financiers, nobles, socialites, and magnates—arrived by private carriage and motorcar, some even escorted by liveried attendants. They strolled aboard via the grand First-Class gangway, their every movement exuding the ease of inherited wealth and cultivated refinement. Within minutes, they were enveloped in a world of sumptuous staterooms, sweeping staircases, and richly appointed salons—a voyage not merely across the Atlantic, but into the lap of luxury.

In stark contrast, the Third-Class passengers—composed primarily of laborers, young families, and wide-eyed immigrants—experienced a different rite of passage. Before boarding, they were directed to medical inspections in accordance with U.S. immigration requirements, where the health of each individual was scrutinized to ensure no communicable diseases would be carried to American shores. These men and women, many of whom had sacrificed all they had for a one-way ticket to the New World, carried with them not finery, but dreams—dreams of farmland, factory work, and futures born from hope rather than inheritance. Though their passage was modest, even austere by comparison, Titanic's Third-Class accommodations far exceeded those of most contemporary liners, offering clean quarters, running water, and structured meal service—luxuries to many who boarded with little more than the clothes on their backs.

Between these two worlds was the Second Class: a space for professionals, teachers, ministers, and skilled tradesmen—those of stable means but not excessive wealth. These passengers were greeted by charming accommodations—comfortable and elegant without the ostentation of First Class. The Second-Class library, smoking room, and promenade offered spaces of refinement and ease, reflecting a growing middle class whose aspirations were as lofty as the ship's highest deck.

As the minutes ticked toward noon, the pier buzzed with the final flurry of dockside activity. Stewards called out last names, porters hauled trunks and valises, and passengers pressed against the rails for a final glimpse of England's coastline. Beneath the ship, mooring lines stretched taut, straining against the inevitability of departure. Then, as the great ship's whistle bellowed—a thunderous, sonorous call that echoed across the harbor—Titanic stirred to life.

At the helm stood Captain Edward John Smith, a man of dignified bearing and long experience. Having served White Star for decades, he was regarded with deep respect and admiration. Whispers among the crew and passengers suggested this would be his final command before a well-earned retirement. While White Star Line officials denied the rumors[91], one must admit that this narrative added an air of ceremony to the journey. Here, in the twilight of a distinguished career, Captain Smith would guide the most advanced ship ever constructed on her inaugural voyage—a culmination of a life spent at sea.

*　*　*

As *Titanic* gracefully glided away from the pier, setting a course towards Cherbourg, France. Amid the familiar routine of departure, Captain Smith's experienced gaze caught sight of the *S.S. City of New York*, a vessel owned by the Inman Line, docked nearby. A sense of déjà vu gripped those who recalled the incident involving the Olympic and the Hawke, both under Captain Smith's command. History seemed poised to repeat itself.

Tension heightened as the City of New York unexpectedly broke free of her moorings and started moving ominously toward the Titanic. An eerie sense of impending disaster loomed over those who remembered past maritime incidents.

---

[91] https://www.bbc.com/news/uk-england-17181461

"We now moved slowly ahead and passed the Teutonic at a creeping pace, but notwithstanding this, the latter strained at her ropes so much that she heeled over several degrees in her efforts to follow the Titanic: the crowd were shouted back, a group of gold-braided officials, probably the harbour-master and his staff, standing on the sea side of the moored ropes, jumped back over them as they drew up taut to a rigid line, and urged the crowd back still farther. But we were just clear, and as we slowly turned the corner into the river I saw the Teutonic swing slowly back into her normal station, relieving the tension alike of the ropes and of the minds of all who witnessed the incident."

~ Lawrence Beesley, 2nd class passenger[92]

The vast size of the Titanic created a powerful displacement of water, drawing smaller ships towards it. It seemed as though a magnetic force emanated from the colossal vessel, pulling not only the City of New York but also other nearby vessels. Yet, the integrity of their lines held firm, preventing a calamity as the ships sailed safely into the vast expanse of open water. The specter of history repeating itself had been averted, thanks to the swift and skillful actions of the maritime crews involved.

* * *

---

[92] https://www.jmilford-titanic.com/2014/05/april-10-1912-new-york-incident.html

As the sun dipped below the western horizon, its amber light spilled across the calm waters of Cherbourg harbor, casting the French port in a golden hue. Against this luminous backdrop, the RMS *Titanic* appeared like a floating palace, her vast hull aglow with lantern light and her four towering funnels etched in silhouette against the fading sky.

Yet for all her majesty, *Titanic* could not dock at the port directly. Her size—unprecedented even by the standards of the age—rendered her incompatible with Cherbourg's piers. Instead, a meticulous and time-honed choreography began, as two tender ships were readied to ferry passengers to the waiting giant anchored offshore.

The S.S. *Nomadic* and S.S. *Traffic*, dwarfed beside the behemoth that was *Titanic*, glided through the harbor like obedient dancers in a grand maritime ballet. Each tender carried a mix of eager travelers: first-class guests in tailored coats and elegant hats, steerage passengers clutching luggage and hope in equal measure, and port officials making their final inspections.

With the new passengers aboard and final cargo secured, *Titanic*'s whistles sounded across the night—a sonorous, commanding note that echoed through the harbor and signaled the continuation of her maiden voyage. She slipped away from the coast of France, the outlines of Cherbourg fading into the night behind her, as she turned westward toward her next stop: Queenstown (now known as Cobb), Ireland.

By the following afternoon, *Titanic* reached the Irish coast under a sky brushed with silver clouds. The quaint port of Queenstown, nestled between green hills and the blue Atlantic, welcomed her arrival. Here, a final flurry of activity unfolded. Seven passengers disembarked—brief but memorable travelers on the great liner—and 120 new ones boarded, joining the ranks of hopeful immigrants, businessmen, and adventurers bound for the promise of America.

The exchange was brisk, the harbor lively with the rhythm of boats and the chatter of onlookers. For those watching from the shore, the Titanic's presence was almost surreal—larger than myth, grander than rumor. Some locals climbed hilltops just for one last glimpse of the ship that had captured the imagination of the world.

Then came the final whistle. The anchor was raised. Lines were drawn in. Titanic slowly drifted away from Queenstown, the sea beneath her glistening like glass, the Irish coastline receding behind her like a fading memory. It was during this moment—graceful and solemn—that the last known photograph of the Titanic was taken. In the image, the ship is framed against the Irish hills, her prow turned toward the open Atlantic, her decks crowded with passengers waving to the distant land they left behind.

The departure was more than a routine maritime ritual—it was the closing of a chapter, the final farewell to the Old World. Aboard the ship, excitement buzzed in dining rooms, corridors, and cabins. Children ran laughing down promenade decks, couples strolled beneath the stars, and letters were penned to loved ones, sealed and stamped with a sense of expectation.

Yet behind the glamour, an invisible shadow had begun to gather.

None on board could have imagined the fate that lay ahead—how the grandeur would give way to struggle, how the joy would be replaced by disbelief. The Titanic, in that serene moment of departure, carried with her more than cargo and dreams. She carried a fragile illusion of invincibility.

As she pushed onward into the Atlantic twilight, slicing

through the cold waters with purpose and poise, her passengers settled in for the journey they believed would end in New York. Their thoughts danced ahead to reunions, opportunities, and new beginnings. But the ocean, timeless and indifferent, had other plans.

The memory of that departure—the peaceful Irish hills fading into the distance, the ship's silhouette against a deepening sky, and the last photograph frozen in time—would linger in history not as a symbol of triumph, but as the final, bittersweet image of a voyage destined to become legend.

One of the Last Photos of Titanic afloat as she leaves Ireland for New York[93]

93 https://www.snopes.com/fact-check/final-photograph-titanic/

10

Chapter 10

Disaster Strikes

April 14th, 1912— *Titanic*, an epitome of luxury and engineering marvel, glided through the tranquil waters of the North Atlantic. The journey had been remarkably peaceful, with the vast ocean appearing as a serene canvas beneath the star-studded sky. The ship, making excellent time, was poised to arrive in New York ahead of schedule. However, this night would bring a shift in the narrative.

In the confined quarters of the wireless room, Morse Code operators Jack Phillips and Harold Bride, diligent employees of the Marconi company, took turns intercepting messages from various vessels in the vicinity. The airwaves crackled with warnings—messages that spoke of an encroaching threat: ice. Though the Marconi operators did not work for White Star Line directly, their allegiance was to the captain, and they dutifully relayed the warnings to the bridge.

As reports of icebergs piled up, Captain Edward Smith decided to alter the Titanic's course, steering the colossal vessel further south in an attempt to navigate around the hazardous ice fields. The urgency in the wireless room heightened as messages flowed in, each one carrying the potential for a life-altering impact. Amidst the flurry of communication, Phillips and Bride found themselves caught in a dilemma—between relaying vital iceberg warnings to the bridge, and attending to the backlog of passenger messages. Only one of these made their company money.

Despite their best efforts, the warnings about icebergs directly in *Titanic's* path, having become somewhat repetitive, were met with nonchalance or, at times, frustration. The enormity of the vessel, coupled with the belief in its unsinkable nature, led to a degree of complacency among some onboard.

As the clock neared 11 PM, a critical message arrived from Wireless Operator Cyril Evans aboard the S.S. *Californian*, a liner positioned approximately 10 miles away from *Titanic*. The *Californian* reported being stopped and surrounded by ice. However, the proximity of the two ships made it challenging for *Titanic's* wireless room to receive the message clearly. Phillips who was manning the radio whilst Bride rested responded:

Keep out; shut up, I'm working: Cape Race

Cyril Evans found himself taken aback by the unexpected backlash in response to his warning. The urgency of the situation was clear to him, but the critical message about being surrounded by ice seemed to fall on deaf ears. With a heavy heart and a sense of impending doom, Evans realized that the time had come to shut off the wireless set and retire for the night. Alone in the Californian's wireless room, he succumbed to the weariness of the long night, leaving the silent room to the whispers of the ocean.

As the night pressed on aboard the Titanic, an air of quietude enveloped the vast expanse of the North Atlantic. High in the crow's nest, lookouts Fredrick Fleet and Renigald Lee strained their eyes in the darkness, their gaze sweeping the tranquil sea for any signs of danger. The eerily calm waters, devoid of the usual rhythmic dance of waves, concealed the lurking hazards that could spell doom for the mighty ship. The moon, which was currently a waning crescent moon, having long since set for the night[94], offered no illumination to aid the vigilant watchmen in their task.

At 11:39 PM, in the midst of this nocturnal stillness, a chilling discovery disrupted the tranquility, a large black void was ahead of them, a telltale signs of an iceberg. The lack of waves and the dim moonlight had conspired to keep this icy threat concealed until it was perilously close. In a heartbeat, the lookouts sounded the alarm, their urgent message echoing through the quiet night, alerting the ship to the impending danger.

First Officer Murdoch, the most senior officer on the bridge at the time, gave orders to turn the ship hard-a-starboard. This was done so as to turn the ship to the left so as to avoid the iceberg, as noted by Walter Lord that turning instructions at

---

[94] https://wgntv.com/weather/weather-blog/sky-conditions-at-the-time-of-the-titanic-disaster/#:~:text=The%20Titanic%20sank%20during%20the,set%20at%204%3A04%20pm.

the time were based on which way the wheel turned, rather than which way the ship turned.[95] This was done so as to perform an S-curve maneuver around the iceberg.[96]

What happened next is actually disputed between accounts. Testimony from surviving officers who had been on the bridge state that Murdoch ordered *Titanic* full astern, which would reverse the engines. However stokers who survived state the order that came on the telegraph was to full stop the ship. Regardless, the next order was to turn hard to port, so as to swing the aft of the ship away from the iceberg. Unfortunately this would prove to not be enough.

It had been 37 seconds since the iceberg was first spotted. *Titanic* collided with the iceberg on her port side. The impact, a thunderous reverberation, sent shockwaves through the ship, buckling plates and tearing apart rivets. Ocean water began to enter and fill the mighty ship, *Titanic's* end had begun.

Expeditions to the wreck later found using ultrasound that six small gashes had been opened up along the side of *Titanic*.[97] This consisted when put together about 12 feet of damage across several watertight compartments. This is in contrast to the conventional thinking following the disaster that a single 300 foot gash had taken down the ship. It had been inconceivable that anything smaller could have sunk *Titanic*.

Even before the ship had fully cleared the iceberg, First officer

---

[95] https://www.telegraph.co.uk/culture/books/booknews/8016752/Titanic-sunk-by-steering-blunder-new-book-claims.html

[96] https://web.archive.org/web/20031028123941/http://www.geocities.com/murdochmystery/Last_Log_of_the_Titanic.html

[97] https://web.archive.org/web/20200831010551/https://www.nytimes.com/1997/04/08/science/toppling-theories-scientists-find-6-slits-not-big-gash-sank-titanic.html?pagewanted=all%2F

Murdoch quickly had the ships watertight doors closed so as to slow any flooding that was the result of the impact. This process took another 30 seconds to fully complete, and contrary to popular belief, crew members were not trapped behind said doors, and alternate routes for escape were provided.

Murdoch was soon joined on the bridge by Captain Smith, who had felt the collision in his cabin, and to whom he gave his initial report on what had happened, and the actions he took. Shortly afterwards, Captain Smith, along with Thomas Andrews, the ships chief architect who have been traveling with a party of guaranteers from Harland & Wolff, headed below deck to inspect the damage.

They found that the forward cargo hold, the mail room, and several boiler rooms were flooded or were flooding. The ballast and bilge pumps were overloaded, and were unable to handle the sheer amount of seawater that was now entering the ship. Andrews would then inform Smith that the first five watertight compartments had been breached. This was more than the ship had been designed to handle, and that the ship would sink within two hours.[98]

* * *

As the gravity of the situation became undeniable, the crew of the Titanic swung into action. At 12:05 AM, Captain Smith orders that the lifeboats to be prepared, only a mere 15 minutes after the fateful collision with the iceberg. Crew soon began

---

[98] Barczewski 2006, p. 148

uncovering and preparing the lifeboats, however it would be another 20 minutes before passengers started boarding said lifeboats. Even then, passengers are reluctant to board, with many not seeing the inherent danger of the ship sinking.

At the same time, Captain Smith had the wireless operators begin to send out a distress signal to any and all ships in the area. The *Frankfurt*, a ship 170 nautical miles away is the first to reply.[99] Several begin to make way to *Titanic*'s last known position, including her sister ship *Olympic*. The *Carpathia*, a Cunard liner, is the closet ship that responds to the distress signal, and quickly makes way towards *Titanic*.

On the boat deck, the evacuation process was underway, and would reflect the societal norms of the time. First and second-class passengers, located closer to the boat deck, were given priority access to the lifeboats. Third-class passengers were held back until the first and second-class were accounted for. This however suggests that the evacuation was calm and orderly, when this was far from the actual truth of what happened.

Different evacuation strategies quickly emerged, with two different officers interpreting the same orders differently. While Second Officer Lightoller only allowed women and children to board lifeboats, adhering to the exact wording of traditional saying "Women and Children first," First Officer Murdoch allowed men to board once nearby women and children were secured.[100] These different clashing strategies created chaos, confusion, and wasted spare room aboard said

---

[99] https://www.britannica.com/story/timeline-of-the-titanics-final-hours

[100] https://adventure.howstuffworks.com/titanic7.htm

lifeboats.

However not all the empty spots in the lifeboats were the result of these differing strategies, as a pervasive problem plagued both, that being the lack of passengers taking the situation seriously. Some treated the aftermath of the collision as a game, with ice falling on the deck resembling a peculiar game of football. Others staggered around in disbelief, failing to board lifeboats until prompted.

This would not however be the only reason for passengers to hesitate boarding the lifeboats. Some simply saw remaining on the sinking *Titanic* to be the safer option, rather than boarding a lifeboat. Many simply did not understand the severity of the situation at hand. To them, the lifeboats look dingy, like they could fall apart at any moment, while the critically crippled *Titanic*, still looked strong and like it would stay afloat, despite it sinking by the head. This along with the differing loading strategies created logistical chaos, and a unwilling to cooperate population, combined with the fact the *Titanic* by design did not have enough lifeboats for everyone, created a deadly situation.

As a result of these various failures, lifeboats left the Titanic only partially filled, and some even departed with shockingly low numbers of passengers. Lifeboat number 1, for instance, left with just 12 occupants. In this case, after the sinking, there were rumors that Sir Cosmo Diff Gordon and his wife Lucy, occupants on board said lifeboat bribed the crew to let them leave and to not go back. Later investigations found this rumor to be unfounded, including the official report into the sinking, though this has not stopped the portrayal of this in media about

Titanic.[101] This combined with the fact the *Titanic* by design did not have enough lifeboats for everyone created a deadly situation.

It should be noted however noted, per testimony from second officer Lightoller, that the true rating of the lifeboats was far less than that of the hypothetical rating.[102] He claimed that under actual conditions, each lifeboat could only probably carry 40 people. If this is to be taken into account, than most of the lifeboats were launched at or near capacity, with several over capacity. Per the official numbers, the only lifeboat to launch above it rated capacity was lifeboat 15.[103]

* * *

It was only as time went on, and as *Titanic* sank lower into the water, that the realization of what was happening hit. People were becoming rowdy, and officers would attempt to keep order. An unfortunate consequence of this was that lifeboats still left the ship partially empty. The *Titanic's* band, amidst the chaos, continued to play music for the public, first in the second-class smoking room, and later on deck, with the legendary story claiming they played "Nearer, My God, to Thee." None of the

[101] https://web.archive.org/web/20141026142857/http://www.biography.com/people/cosmo-duff-gordon-283836

[102] Gittins, Dave; Akers-Jordan, Cathy; Behe, George (2011). "Too Few Boats, Too Many Hindrances". In Halpern, Samuel (ed.). *Report into the Loss of the SS* Titanic: *A Centennial Reappraisal*. Stroud, UK: The History Press. ISBN 978-0-7524-6210-3.

[103] https://www.titanicpages.com/lifeboat/15

band members survived the sinking.

Lifeboat after lifeboat left the ship, things began to become chaotic, and several men tried to board the lifeboats, even as they were being lowered, with some being forced back off at gunpoint. At one point, lifeboat 13, after being launched, drifted under the descending lifeboat 15, and was nearly crushed.

The second to last lifeboat, Collapsible Boat C, was lowered into the frigid waters with 40 people on board, including J. Bruce Ismay, chairman of the White Star Line. Ismay's decision to board a lifeboat, despite his involvement in the evacuation efforts, earned him criticism and the enduring moniker "J. Brute Ismay."[104] This image of Ismay as a coward or brute however has been challenged in more recent years, long after the disaster.

The last lifeboat to be successfully launched would be Collapsible Boat D, with 20 people onboard, at 2:05 AM. At 2:10 AM, and attempt was made to retrieve Collapsible Boat B from its storage spot, however this failed when it landed upside down on the boat deck. The ocean, having by now reached said boat deck, soon washed the upside-down lifeboat off the sinking ship at 2:15 AM.

At the same time, Collapsible Boat A, the last lifeboat, was also being prepared, but that too was soon washed off the ship. Several people would jump into the water to attempt to board the lifeboat, however as the sides were not pulled up yet, it soon filled with water. Due to hypothermia, of the people who climbed into the half sunken lifeboat, only about 14 survived.[105] Lifeboat 14 would later rescue the passengers

---

[104] https://www.encyclopedia-titanica.org/titanic-lifeboat-c/

[105] https://titanicfacts.net/titanic-lifeboats/

onboard the partially sunken lifeboat. With all the lifeboats gone or away 1500 people now we're stuck on a sinking ship with nowhere to go.

Titanic only has minutes left, as the bow sinks further and further into the water. Reports from survivors claim Captain Smith calmly stood on the bridge as his ship went down. His role in the disaster and the subsequent evacuation is often debated, as this was the first and only major disaster of his career while in charge. They mainly argue over whether the disorganized evacuation was his fault, or that of his officers. This comes if his delegation of authority absolves him of wrong doing, or if his possible lack of oversight resulting in conflicting policies resulted in less people being saved.

* * *

Those who remained onboard could harbor a guess that the end was near. Titanic was groaning, as the metal strained under the stress as water rapidly filled the bow, with it already up to the boat deck. No lifeboats were left, and for those passengers left behind, there only hope was that *Titanic* could stay afloat long enough for help to arrive.

On the lifeboats, many attempted to get as far away from the sinking ship as possible to avoid being sucked down by it. This was a common wisdom of the sea at the time, and one that was of high concern for experienced seamen.

For the freezing passengers on said lifeboats, they could only watch in horror as *Titanic* sank further and further into the abyss. Soon they knew the end was near, when suddenly they lost sight of the great ocean liner. Water had reached the generators, and *Titanic* soon lost power. It must be remembered that there was no moon that night, and the ocean was calm. The same conditions that hid the iceberg until the last moment now hid *Titanic* herself.

As the *Titanic* lost power and darkness enveloped the ship, the relentless pull of the sinking became more evident, if only audibly. Loose objects slid forward with resounding crashes, and the mighty vessel ultimately split into two, though many survivors disputed this at the time. This was a result of the conditions at the time of the split, as *Titanic* had just lost power, and of those who could see the ship and survived, their eyes had not time to adjust to the darkness. It is no wonder that many reported that the ship sank in one piece, as of those who did survive, few could see it split in two.

Regardless, the facts remain that at 2:20 AM, the stern of *Titanic* slipped beneath the icy Atlantic waters. 1500 people found themselves being plunged into the frigid waters. At only 28 degrees Fahrenheit/-2 degrees Celsius[106], survival chances were bleak due to the plummeting temperatures in water that was only liquid due to its salt content. Additionally, the lifeboats hesitated to return to pick up survivors from the water, fearing that their small would swamp in the chaos. Hypothermia wound up claiming the lives of hundreds, some in as little as 15 minutes.

Some survivors sought refuge on Collapsible Lifeboat B, which had overturned during launching. They stood on top

---

[106] https://cruise.blog/2024/02/titanic-water-temperature#:~:text=When%20the%20Titanic%20hit%20the,)%2C%20which%20is%20below%20freezing.

of the boat throughout the night, sinking lower as its air pocket dissipated. Notable individuals on this precarious refuge included Second Officer Lightoller, Chief Baker Charles Joughin, and Wireless Operator Harold Bride. Some accounts claim that Captain Smith had swam up near the stricken lifeboat but left when he saw it was full. These claims are impossible to verify, and his last known verified location was standing on the bridge of the Titanic as she went down. Passengers on board this lifeboats would be rescued later by other lifeboats, surviving since they were only partially submerged in the water.

After a reorganization of passengers on the lifeboats, two of them did return were post of the passengers in the water were. These were lifeboats 14 and 4, and in all they found only 9 people were still alive, with three dying shortly after being pulled from the water.[107] Lifeboat 14 would also take on passengers from Collapsible boat A, which was close to sinking due to not being properly deployed.

Once those in the water succumbed to hypothermia, there was only silence. In the hours between the sinking of *Titanic*, and the arrival of *Carpathia*, shocked passengers could only wait, with only each other and their own thoughts for company. They were the only living beings for miles around, and were in dingy little boats in the middle of the Atlantic, having gone through a dramatic experience. Thanks to the efforts of the Marconi operators, help was on its way.

---

[107] https://rmstitanic1912.weebly.com/waiting-to-be-rescued.html

Chapter 11

Messages into the Void

Reversing the clock a bit, we return to *Titanic's* wireless room, moments after the Ship hit the iceberg. At 12:05 AM, Captain Smith had asked the wireless operators Harold Bride and Jack Phillips to begin to send out a distress signal to anyone in the area that could listen. Dutifully, the two began to do as asked, and began sending out a distress signal over the airwaves into the cold Void of the Atlantic. The two would take turns sending out the distress messages.

In a snap decision, Phillips and Bride together, decided to use the well-known CQD in their messages, due to their familiarity with it instead of the newly designated emergency signal of SOS. They were not alone in this regard either, as CQD remained especially popular among British vessels.

However, in what can only be described as a moment of gallows humor, one of the two did suggest trying the newer

SOS signal instead, humorously acknowledging that it might be their last opportunity to use it. Amid the flickering lights and the rhythmic tapping of the telegraph, the operators alternated between CQD and SOS throughout the night. The messages carried across the ocean, reaching out for aid from any vessel within earshot:

> "Come at once. We have struck a berg. It's a CQD, old man. Position 41.46 N 50.14 W."[108]

At 12:21 AM, a crucial response crackled through the airwaves from the Cunard liner *Carpat*liner only a mere 53 miles away and heading east to the Mediterranean[109]. The urgency in their exchange reflected the escalating crisis:

> *"I say old man, do you know there is a batch of messages coming through for you from MCC."*
> "CQD CQD."
> "Shall I tell my captain? Do you require assistance?"
> "Yes, come quick!"[110]

---

[108] https://www.theatlantic.com/technology/archive/2012/04/the-technology-that-allowed-the-titanic-survivors-to-survive/255848/

[109] https://www.britannica.com/topic/Carpathia

[110] https://www.theatlantic.com/technology/archive/2012/04/the-technology-that-allowed-the-titanic-survivors-to-survive/255848/

Harold Cottam, the wireless operator on the *Carpathia*, rushed to deliver the message to the crew on bridge currently in charge. Initially met with skepticism, Cottam persisted, and soon hurried to Captain Rostron's quarters, waking him with the dire news. Upon comprehending the severity of the situation, Captain Rostron ordered the *Carpathia* to alter course towards the Titanic's last known position.[111]

"Putting about and heading for you."

* * *

Several hundred miles away onboard *Titanic's* sister ship *Olympic*, the Marconi wireless operators were in for a dire surprise as the distress signal reached them. The on duty wireless operator at the time, Erie Moore quickly raced to awaken his coworker Alec Bagot with the news. *Titanic* was sinking.[112]

By Mr. Bagot's own account in a record preserved by the Titanic Historical Society, he stated he thought that this declaration from his coworker was a joke at first. Often the two would joke about another ship sinking, namely that of the *Lusitania* or *Mauritania* due to those ships being owned by White Star Line's chief rival Cunard, even if the two didn't actually work

[111] https://www.titanicinquiry.org/USInq/AmInq01Rostron01.php

[112] https://titanichistoricalsociety.org/i-heard-titanics-call/

for White Star. However, in this instance, this notion would soon be banished, as Mr. Moore made it clear that this was no joke.

Writing down the distress signal from *Titanic*, Mr. Moore soon sent Mr. Bagot in search of *Olympics'* captain, Herbert Haddock, carrying a sealed envelope with the message in hand. He soon found himself on the bridge with the captain and the first Officer, where he handed over the note.

After quickly reading the message, Captain Haddock made his decision. Grabbing a notepad, he quickly scribbled down a message and told Mr. Baggot to take it back to the wireless room to transmit. Captain Haddock had written the following message to be sent to *Titanic*:

Commander Titanic Am lighting up all possible boilers as fast as I can – Haddock.' [sic]

After handing the new message to Mr. Baggot, Captain Haddock then instructed that he bring him any news in regards to *Titanic*. The young wireless operator was then sworn to secrecy by the captain, so as to tell no other soul aboard on what was going on. As Mr. Baggot made his way back to the wireless room, *Olympic* began to turn around,

* * *

Several miles away from *Titanic* sat the *S.S Californian*, having

116

stopped for the night due to packs of ice surrounding the ship. Several officers on board the ship noted the appearance of rockets on the horizon, apparently coming from the much larger vessel they could see in that location. Hurriedly they went to wake the captain of the *Californian*, Stanley Lord for guidance.

Captain Lord, upon being informed of the situation, suggested the rockets were simply company signals from one company ship to another one it owned[113]. He did however suggest to attempt To make contact with the vessel via Morse Lamp. It was reported by some of the crew after the fact that they thought the rockets could indicate a vessel under distress, though the validity of this has some doubt.

Either way, it was noted that no response was received from *Titanic* to *Californian*, and now further attempt at contact was made, nor was any attempt made to wake the wireless operator to attempt contact that way. It should however be noted that wireless technology was still new at the time, and was not fully trusted or at the forefront in the mind of many captains. Additional research published by British Historian Tim Maltin via the Smithsonian[114], concludes that Captain Lord erroneously determined the ship on the horizon was the not the *Titanic* due to its appearance being much smaller than expected, and knowing *Titanic* would have been the only other ship in the area with a wireless, concluded the ship they saw had none. When the rockets stopped firing and the lights disappeared, it

[113] https://owlcation.com/humanities/The-SS-Californian-The-Ship-That-Ignored-Titanics-Distress-Calls

[114] https://www.smithsonianmag.com/science-nature/did-the-titanic-sink-because-of-an-optical-illusion-102040309/

was assumed the ship they were observing had sailed away.

After combing weather reports from the time, it was concluded by Maltin that due to current temperatures and weather, and optical illusion that made the horizon appear higher than it was, was responsible for *Titanic* appearing smaller than expected. This is also further likely an explanation for *Californian* receiving no response via Morse Lamp, with either *Titanic* not seeing the initial contact in the first place, or it's response not being seen by *Californian*. Either way, either due to these factors, or all of them, not action was taken by the *Californian*, with the crew not learning if the disaster until the ships wireless operator, Cyril Evans, awoke in the morning.

* * *

Onboard the *Carpathia*, the urgency of the rescue mission it had taken manifested in a flurry of coordinated activity aboard the ship. The crew, displaying unwavering professionalism and dedication, swiftly implemented a comprehensive plan to address the impending crisis. Hot water was turned off to the passenger cabins, and extra stokers were awoken and mobilized to ensure the engines operated at maximum capacity, providing the *Carpathia* with the necessary speed to reach the stricken Titanic in record time. So fast in fact, it had broken the max speed for which the ship was rated, which was 14.5 knots, and instead made the journey at 17 knots instead.[115]

---

[115] https://www.history.com/news/5-things-you-may-not-know-about-tit anics-rescue-ship

Inside the ship, cabins and dining rooms were hastily being transformed into makeshift sanctuaries, ready to welcome the survivors from the ill-fated *Titanic*. Blankets were unfurled, warm beverages prepared from areas where hot water still worked, and medical supplies readied to attend to the needs of those who would soon come aboard the *Carpathia*.

"Icebergs loomed up and fell astern and we never slackened. It was an anxious time with the Titanic's fateful experience very close in our minds. There were 700 souls on Carpathia and those lives as well as the survivors of the Titanic herself depended on the sudden turn of the wheel."

-Captain Arthur H. Rostron, Commander of Carpathia[116]

With heightened vigilance, additional lookouts were also stationed atop the *Carpathia's* decks, scanning the darkness for any signs of obstacles or hazards that might impede their progress. As the ship got closer to Titanic, this became more and more necessary as the same ice that had stricken the larger vessel began to appear. It would not do for *Carpathia* to strike an iceberg as well. In a display of foresight and preparedness, *Carpathia's* own lifeboats were made ready for deployment Just in case, for use possible use in the impending rescue effort. Each boat, meticulously inspected and manned by skilled seamen, awaited the critical task of retrieving survivors

---

[116] https://thetitanicnhdproject.weebly.com/quotes-from-survivors.htmlo

from the lifeboats and debris scattered across the icy waters.

Even as the *Carpathia* surged forward at a speed not thought possible for the ship, it still took three and a half agonizing hours for the ship to reach the Titanic's location. Until it arrived, the wireless operator, Harold Cottam, could only listen to the diminishing signals emanating from the *Titanic's* wireless room as water gradually encroached upon the generators.

> "Come as quickly as possible old man: our engine-room is filling up to the boilers."

At 2 AM, the last haunting message pierced the airwaves:

> "Come quick. Engine room nearly full,"[117]

Though no one listening in at the time knew it exactly, only minutes later, *Titanic* fully slipped beneath the waves of the North Atlantic.

---

[117] https://www.bbc.com/news/magazine-17631595

Chapter 12

Aftermath & Investigation

Despite her crews best efforts, it would not be until 4 AM when The *Carpathia* finally arrived to the scene of the disaster. By this point, *Titanic* was now at the bottom of the ocean, 2.4 miles below them. The only thing left was lifeboats, debris, and bodies. *Carpathia* was now resigned to the challenging task of picking up the 706 survivors[118], a number vastly different from *Titanic*'s departure number of 2,240.

In the hours between the sinking and the arrival of The *Carpathia*, two lifeboats had been organized to go back and try to find any survivors among the wreckage. Only Six were found alive, with one dying shortly afterwards. In the United States inquiry to the sinking, Seaman Frank O. Evans described the scene:

---

[118] https://titanicfacts.net/titanic-survivors/how-many-people-survived/

Senator Smith: Any dead?

Mr. Evans: One died on the way back, sir. There were plenty of dead bodies about us.

Senator Smith: How many? Scores of them?

Mr. Evans: You couldn't hardly count them, sir. I was afraid to look over the sides because it might break my nerves down.[119]

In the stark light of day, the aftermath of the tragedy unfolded. An iceberg, stained with the red paint of the Titanic, bore witness to the catastrophic event that had unfolded in the darkened depths of the North Atlantic. The sinking of the Titanic left an indelible mark on history, forever altering the perception of maritime safety and punctuating the end of an era. By 8 AM, it had completed the rescue mission. Meanwhile, the *Californian*, having arrived belatedly, continued to search for survivors as the *Carpathia* headed back to New York.

By 9 AM, the *Carpathia*, now laden with the rescued passengers, turned resolutely on its course, steering towards the bustling metropolis of New York. The ship carried not only the survivors but also the weight of an unprecedented tragedy that had sent shockwaves across the globe. The ocean liner, once a vessel of leisure and luxury, now bore witness to the collective trauma of those who had escaped the clutches of the icy abyss.

At the request of White Star Line's chair, J. Bruce Ismay, who had survived the sinking, the following was sent to the company offices:

---

[119] https://www.encyclopedia-titanica.org/titanic-where-were-the-bodies.html

"Deeply regret advise you Titanic sank this morning,
after collision with iceberg, resulting in serious loss
of life. Full particulars later."[120]

Meanwhile, the *Olympic*, having responded promptly to the distress signals, was directed to forge ahead on its intended voyage to Europe. This decision aimed to shield the already traumatized survivors from the unsettling sight of another sister ship, sparing them further emotional distress in the wake of their harrowing experience.

Three days later, the *Carpathia* glided into New York Harbor, a symbol of both relief and grief. The sight of the ship stirred a whirlwind of emotions among the waiting families—hopeful anticipation for news of their loved ones, the insatiable curiosity of the public eager for details, and the ominous presence of federal subpoenas awaiting J. Bruce Ismay, the controversial figure at the heart of the Titanic's tragedy.

Official investigations conducted both in America and by British Committees, showered praise upon Captain Rostron for his heroic role in the rescue operation. His decisive and compassionate actions in the face of adversity earned him accolades and underscored the valor that had defined the *Carpathia's* mission that fateful night.

On the contrary, J. Bruce Ismay, found himself ensnared in a web of public condemnation. Accused of cowardice for allegedly securing a place in a lifeboat reserved for women and children, Ismay became a pariah in the court of public opinion. Faced

---

[120] https://www.smithsonianmag.com/history/titanic-sank-this-morning-1 02770115/

with intense scrutiny, he opted for a life of relative obscurity, withdrawing from the public eye for the remainder of his days.

* * *

The tale of the *Carpathia's* valiant rescue effort, intricately woven into the aftermath of the Titanic disaster, unfolded as a poignant chapter in maritime history. Captain Rostron's exemplary leadership aboard the *Carpathia* stood in stark contrast to the tarnished reputation of White Star Line's managing director, J. Bruce Ismay. This stark dichotomy mirrored the intricate and often conflicting nature of human responses in the face of an unprecedented catastrophe. As the *Carpathia* sailed into the solemn embrace of New York Harbor, its decks bore witness not only to survivors seeking solace but also to the indelible scars of a night destined to linger in the collective memory of humanity.

* * *

The investigations that unfolded in the aftermath of the Titanic sinking were a testament to the collective shock and public outcry that reverberated globally. Long before the survivors found solace in the sanctuary of New York City aboard the *Carpathia*, the gears of inquiry were set in motion, reflecting the urgency and gravity of the tragedy.

At the helm of the United States Senate inquiry stood Senator

Alden Smith, a figure renowned for his pioneering work in crafting railroad safety laws. With a sense of urgency, he orchestrated a comprehensive investigation that sometimes appeared more like a one-man blame game than a collaborative effort. Among those summoned was J. Bruce Ismay, the figurehead of the International Mercantile Marine and the White Star Line, who had initially intended to return to the United Kingdom.

Survivors, along with executives from White Star Line and IMM, found themselves in the witness stand, their testimonies weaving a complex narrative of events leading to the disaster. The final report, unveiled on May 28, 1912, placed blame on Captain Edward Smith for displaying indifference to the reported ice fields and identified inadequate safety practices. The British Board of Trade, responsible for regulations concerning required lifeboats, also bore a share of accountability.

Blame was also placed on Stanley Lord, Captain of *The Californian*, to not responding to *Titanic*'s distress signal. It was determined by the inquiry, on account of testimony officers and crew aboard *The Californian* that the ship had only been roughly 10 miles from *Titanic*'s last known position. The inquiry would ultimately ruin Captain Lord's maritime carer and reputation.

Some however purport that Captain Lord and *The Californian* should not have reviewed the blame that it did. In a 1992 paper by Lt. Cmdr. Craig McLean and David Eno, they determined that testimony against Captain Lord was faulty and that the number the committee used were in error.[121]

While J. Bruce Ismay faced scrutiny during the inquiry, no

---

[121] The Case for Captain Lord https://www.usni.org/magazines/naval-history-magazine/1992/march/case-captain-lord

violations of maritime laws or regulations were found against him regarding issues such as the proximity to the Californian. The Titanic disaster was ultimately deemed an act of God due to the collision with the iceberg, but the intricacies surrounding the incident prompted the implementation of new laws and maritime regulations.

These regulations, etched into maritime history, included provisions for an adequate number of lifeboats for all passengers, reduced speed in ice-prone areas, disciplined use of rockets for emergencies only, regular lifeboat drills, and the maintenance of 24/7 wireless radio operators. These measures, implemented in the years following the Titanic disaster, became foundational pillars of maritime safety, ensuring that the lessons learned from the tragedy would serve as a beacon for future generations navigating the world's oceans.

J. Bruce Ismay, despite returning to lead the White Star Line, adopted a low profile due to public criticism of his survival while many others perished. The subsequent merger of White Star Line with Cunard resulted in the formation of White Star Cunard Line, eventually finding a new home under the umbrella of Carnival Cruises. Today, the White Star name endures as a premium service brand on Cunard ships, a subtle reminder of a bygone era in maritime history.

The Titanic disaster's profound impact went beyond regulatory changes; it played a pivotal role in shaping the very essence of maritime safety. While other shipwrecks had occurred, such as the sinking of the Empress of Ireland, it was the unprecedented death toll, particularly among the wealthy, and the loss of a notable U.S. official that elevated the Titanic's significance in the annals of maritime safety regulations. The lessons learned from the tragedy continue to resonate, ensuring that the legacy of the Titanic lives on as a beacon for maritime safety and accountability.

Chapter 13

Public Fascination & the Media

Despite the immediate shock and grief it caused, the sinking of the *Titanic* did not retain a prominent place in the public imagination for much of the 20th century outside the initial fervor following the sinking.

While the tragedy certainly left a lasting mark on survivors and families of the victims, its broader cultural impact faded relatively quickly in the years after 1912. Outside of the initial fervor surrounding the disaster, the Titanic's story existed largely in the background—overshadowed by other events, including maritime catastrophes with more pressing political or military implications.

For many, the *Titanic* remained a subject of niche interest. It was a notable event, yes, but not yet the universal symbol of hubris, heroism, and human vulnerability it would later become. It is actually Walter Lord, author of the book *A Night to*

Remember, that is credited with renewing public interest in the event.[122] Even then, Mr. Lord has stated he was inspired by his own memories of a voyage aboard *Titanic's* sister ships *Olympic*, rather than interest in *Titanic* directly.

> *It's a funny thing, but today the Titanic is probably much more – that is people are much more aware of it than they were in 1954, when I was doing my research.*
> *~ Walter Lord*[123]

It can be argued that *Titanic's* rise to lasting cultural prominence came not directly from the tragedy itself, but rather through a gradual buildup—one shaped heavily by film, literature, and eventually was cemented with the discovery of the wreck in 1986.

In fact, other maritime disasters captured more attention in the decades immediately following the *Titanic's* sinking. The 1915 torpedoing of the *Lusitania* during World War I, for example, had a far greater impact on international politics and public sentiment, particularly in the United States. With its comparable loss of life and its role in shifting American opinion toward entering the war, the *Lusitania* overshadowed the *Titanic* in public discourse. While the *Titanic* was mourned as a tragic accident, the *Lusitania* was seen as an outrage—its sinking a deliberate act of aggression in a world already consumed by

---

[122] https://oceanlinersmagazine.com/2020/10/08/wlord/#:~:text=The%20first%20paperback%20edition%20was,on%20her%20sister%20ship%2C%20Olympic.

[123] https://www.azquotes.com/quote/1017549#google_vignette

conflict.[124]

What *Titanic* did provide however, was good cinema. As with pretty much any disaster, public interest in everything *Titanic* was immense. In the immediate months following the disaster, any footage of the ship or her crew where highly sought after. To the point that some footage from other ships was faked as from being from *Titanic* so as to make a quick buck.[125] Not all of it was done in bad faith of course, especially as time went on. But with the sinking of *Titanic* being a peace time disaster, it's hard not to see this an an opportunity to tell the ultimate tragedy, free of outside causes except human ones. Basically, it is the perfect drama film.

* * *

Early attempts to dramatize the *Titanic* story on film were swift to come into fruition. The first was *Saved from the Titanic* (1912), released just a month after the disaster. Starring Dorothy Gibson, a real survivor of the sinking, the film was both a historical artifact and a raw attempt at emotional processing. If this film was meant to make money for the distributor, well that should be obvious. For Gibson however, this film may have been away to process her trauma at the time, evidenced by her helping write the script, and willingness to join the

---

[124] https://gillpaulauthor.wordpress.com/2015/06/06/why-do-we-rememb er-the-titanic-but-not-the-lusitania/

[125] https://silentology.wordpress.com/2015/04/26/lost-films-saved-from-t he-titanic-1912/

project so soon after the disaster. Her actual mindset however is unknown.

> *"Saved from the Titanic," featuring Miss Dorothy Gibson, who is a survivor of the wreck. This picture does not show anything of a sensational nature, but is a good, clean patriotic picture; also gives you the opportunity of seeing Miss Gibson in the stellar role. Don't miss it.*
> *~ Review from the Chickasha Daily Express, May 20, 1912, page 3*[126]

Unfortunately, this film is now considered a lost film, having been destroyed in a fire, and surviving today only in production stills and written accounts.

---

[126] https://blog.genealogybank.com/dorothy-gibsons-real-life-movie-saved-from-the-titanic.html

Poster for the film "Saved From The Titanic" (1912)[127]

Over the decades, filmmakers continued to revisit the story, each with their own interpretation. One of the more unusual entries came during World War II with the German film *Titanic* (1943), produced under the Nazi regime. Though intended as anti-British propaganda, the film's tone and message proved so unsettling that it was banned by German authorities shortly after completion. It is also rumored that Joseph Goebbels had the director executed, after he was found dead in his cell.[128]

In the film, a fictional German Officer named Peterson, is shown as the protagonist in the face of greasy capitalists who will do anything to increase their own wealth and stock price. It portrayed the Germans as calm and collected, while it condemned the English. The film cost four million Reichmarks, equivalent to 180 million United States Dollars as of 2025.[129] the film would not be shown in Germany until 1949, and was banned in the west, but was allowed to premiere in the east by the Soviets due to its anti-capitalist message.

Tragically, the ship used for the filming in place of the *Titanic*, the *Cap Arcona*, was used as a prison ship as part of the holocaust, housing up to 7,000 prisoners from the Neuengamme concentration camp.[130] On May 3rd, 1945, the *Cap Arcona* was bombed and sunk by the RAF, who had been under the impression the ship was being used by SS and high ranking Nazi officials to escape a collapsing Germany. As

---

[127] https://www.imdb.com/title/tt0002475/

[128] https://www.cruiselinehistory.com/nazi-titanic-movie-80th-anniversary-of-the-ww-2-epic-never-released-in-germany/

[129] https://collider.com/nazi-titanic-movie/

[130] https://www.washingtonpost.com/history/2022/12/18/germany-titanic-film-disaster/

a result, planes also shot at survivors in the water after the sinking. Only 350 of those onboard survived, a death toll far higher than that of the *Titanic* disaster itself.

Interestingly enough, at the time of writing, this film has a 60 percent score on the review site Rotten Tomatoes from critics[131]. Despite its complicated legacy, the production values were notable, and some of its footage was later repurposed in more widely respected adaptations.

---

[131] https://www.rottentomatoes.com/m/1133451-titanic

Poster for Titanic (1943), a German propaganda film[132]

---

[132] https://www.imdb.com/de/title/tt0036443/reviews/

One such adaptation, A Night to Remember (1958), became the definitive portrayal of the disaster for several generations. Based on Walter Lord's acclaimed book of the same name, the film was praised for its historical accuracy, restraint, and respect for the real-life figures involved. Although some fictionalized elements were added, mainly for dramatic purposes, this movie is still praised for its accuracy for what was.known at the time. For many years, it remained the most authoritative visual representation of the *Titanic* story.

It has been admitted after the fact, and acknowledged by groups such as the Criterion Collection, that a desire to "get things right" are reasons for this films staying power.[133] That this is what makes it a timeless classic, despite some of its fictional elements. It sought to make people remember that this was an actual tragedy, during a period in which interest was at an all time low. Though it succeeded in its goal to increase interest in the event for a short time, it still ended up waning for several decades, though interest did remain better than before the film came out.

---

[133] https://www.criterion.com/current/posts/29-a-night-to-remember?srsl
tid=AfmBOorkG1B6176z-TKupRZVxWNvz6T5s96RVw9oP-IkysU3JEZSBC
Wp

Poster for "A Night To Remember" (1958)[134]

Another significant film, though one completely fictional, *Raise the Titanic* (1980), imagined a speculative future where the ship was brought back to the surface. Although a financial failure, the movie reflected a growing curiosity about the wreck itself— curiosity that culminated in the successful 1985 expedition by oceanographer Robert Ballard, when he found the ships wreck. The images of the *Titanic* lying on the ocean floor, remarkably preserved after more than seven decades despite being broke. In two, reignited worldwide interest. The ship was no longer just a historical event—it was real, tangible, and visually stunning in its final resting place.

This rediscovery set the stage for the most culturally influential portrayal of all: James Cameron's *Titanic* (1997). Combining historical recreation with fictional romance, the film reached a massive global audience, breaking box office records and winning eleven Academy Awards. Its success wasn't simply due to spectacle—it tapped into timeless themes of love, loss, and human vulnerability.[135] For many viewers, it was their first introduction to the real story behind the *Titanic*, and it sparked a massive wave of renewed interest in the history of the ship and its passengers.

---

[134] https://www.imdb.com/title/tt0051994/reviews/

[135] https://heritageherald.com/2023/03/01/why-titanic-works/

Poster for James Cameron's Titanic (1997); image credit to Disney/Paramount pictures[136]

In the years since, the *Titanic* has maintained a firm place in popular culture. Exhibitions of artifacts recovered from the wreck draw millions. Documentaries continue to analyze new theories about the sinking. Books and educational programs revisit the disaster from every conceivable angle—engineering, sociology, psychology, and even ethics. The *Titanic* has evolved from a sunken ship into a symbol: of ambition, of technological overconfidence, of the unpredictable power of nature.

Part of what makes the *Titanic's* story so enduring is that it reflects a universal human tension—our desire to master the world around us, and the consequences of overreach. While the disaster did lead to meaningful maritime safety reforms, such as improved lifeboat regulations and mandatory 24-hour radio communication, these practical outcomes are only a small part of the legacy. The broader cultural memory of the *Titanic* is built on emotion, symbolism, and narrative.

Today, the *Titanic* is no longer just a historical event. It has become a canvas onto which we project our fears, our dreams, and our fascination with the past. It is studied not just by historians, but by artists, filmmakers, and writers. In death, the Titanic has achieved what it never did in life—a kind of immortality, carried forward not just in the cold statistics of its sinking, but in the imagination of generations.

---

[136] https://www.imdb.com/it/title/tt0120338/

14

Chapter 14

Discovery

In the wake of the *Titanic* sinking, a series of ambitious endeavors were launched in a quest to find and salvage the ill-fated vessel. Early proposals for salvage, which bordered on the unconventional, included the use of dynamite, balloons, and giant electromagnets. However, these innovative ideas were eventually discarded due to technological limitations and the outbreak of World War I, which diverted resources away from such ventures.

The 1960s and 70s ushered in a renewed era of exploration and pursuit of the *Titanic* wreckage. The Titanic Salvage Company emerged, bringing forth audacious proposals such as filling the wreck with ping pong balls, deploying nitrogen balloons, and even attempting to turn it into an iceberg to facilitate its ascent to the surface. Despite these grand plans, the sheer enormity of the undertaking and the exorbitant estimated costs, pegged at a minimum of a quarter of a billion dollars, led to the eventual demise of the Titanic Salvage Company.[137]

Expeditions in the ensuing years shifted their focus from salvaging the Titanic to the more modest goal of discovery. Plans for a joint expedition by Disney and the National Geographic Society were shelved due to the prohibitive estimated costs.

Consequently, the quest for the Titanic shifted hands to wealthy individuals and businesses seeking both exploration and publicity. The eccentric oil billionaire Jack Grimm made three attempts to find the wreck, employing unconventional methods that ranged from utilizing a trained monkey named Titan[138], to underwater scanning technology. Unfortunately, his efforts were plagued by technical setbacks.

Mr. Grimm would make three major expeditions to the area in which Titanic sank so as to locate the wreck in 1980, 1981, and 1983.[139] The first expedition ended in failure, only determining there was metal on the ocean floor, but did not know if it was natural or man made.

The second expedition sought to build off the lessons learned from the first one. Using much better equipment, most of the searched targets appeared to be natural. However one appeared to be man-made, with Grimm declaring it to be the propeller blade of the *Titanic*. His claims would be dismissed at large as incorrect, though interestingly, it was later determined that

[137] https://www.history.co.uk/articles/outrageous-schemes-to-raise-the-titanic

[138] https://www.mentalfloss.com/history/titanic/jack-grimm-explorer-titanic-bigfoot

[139] https://www.titanicconnections.com/wreck/jack-grimm-titanic-expedition-1980-1981-1983/

his equipment did pass near the stern of the *Titanic*, but failed to detect it.[140]

The third attempt, so as to locate the "propeller blade" again ended in early failure to weather. When the wreck was actually discovered two years later, Grimm tried to take credit, but was largely dismissed out of hand.

* * *

The pivotal moment in the search for the *Titanic* was marked by the unwavering determination of Dr. Robert Ballard. His relentless quest, which began in 1977, faced initial setbacks, but Ballard persisted as technological advancements offered new possibilities. In 1982, the United States Navy provided funding for Ballard's submersible, initially intended for investigating the wrecks of the USS *Thresher* and *Scorpion*.[141] Recognizing a unique opportunity, Ballard seized the moment and secured permission to search for the Titanic during this mission with any time left over. It was a crucial turning point that set the stage for the historic discovery.

Finally, in 1985, armed with the lessons learned from previous searches, advancements in technology, and his own lessons learned while searching for the navy submarines,

---

[140] https://www.titanicbelfast.com/history-of-titanic/titanic-stories/finding-titanic-from-search-to-seabed/

[141] https://www.nationalgeographic.co.uk/history-and-civilisation/2018/11/titanic-was-found-during-secret-cold-war-navy-mission

Ballard successfully located the long-lost Titanic. [142] This groundbreaking achievement not only unveiled the resting place of the iconic ocean liner but also revolutionized the approach to discovering shipwrecks, setting new standards for underwater exploration.

> *"Now I understood what had happened. The heavier objects go straight down. The lighter objects sink at a slower rate, and prevailing currents carry them farther away. In Thresher's case, the debris field stretched for roughly a mile. It seems like common sense, but it's not the kind of thing you think about until you see it. The key to finding sunken ships was to search for the long debris trail and follow it back to the vessel. This was the great lesson Thresher taught me—and one that would soon help me immensely."*
> — *Dr. Robert D. Ballard*[143]

---

[142] https://www.whoi.edu/know-your-ocean/ocean-topics/ocean-human-lives/underwater-archaeology/rms-titanic/1985-discovery-of-rms-titanic/

[143] https://www.goodreads.com/author/quotes/39604.Robert_D._Ballard

Dr. Robert Ballard[144]

* * *

The discovery triggered a tidal wave of public interest, transforming the Titanic site into a global tourist attraction. Tickets and expedition packages, priced at a premium, became coveted commodities as celebrities, historians, and enthusiasts alike sought the opportunity to witness the haunting remains of the once-grand vessel lying in the depths of the North Atlantic. The site's newfound popularity transcended geographical boundaries, creating a cultural phenomenon that captured the collec-

---

[144] https://www.titanicbelfast.com/history-of-titanic/titanic-stories/robert-ballard-the-man-behind-rms-titanic-discovery/

tive imagination.

The late 1980s and early 1990s witnessed an unprecedented surge in public fascination with the Titanic wreck. The haunting images and stories from the depths resonated with a global audience, fueling a renewed interest in maritime history. The wreck became a symbol of both the triumphs and tragedies of human ambition, a tangible reminder of the fragility of technological marvels in the face of nature's forces.

The cultural impact of the Titanic discovery extended well into the 1990s and early 2000s. Documentaries, books, and films further immortalized the story of the doomed ocean liner, solidifying its place in popular culture. The mystique surrounding the Titanic continued to captivate audiences, and the wreck's allure persisted as a testament to the enduring power of exploration and the profound connection between humanity and the sea.

The transformation of the *Titanic* from a tragic maritime disaster into a lucrative tourist destination sparked a wave of efforts to salvage artifacts from its resting place on the ocean floor. This endeavor, however, was not without its ethical dilemmas, as the appropriateness of disturbing a site of such historical and emotional significance came under scrutiny. The debate extended across various stakeholders, encompassing explorers, preservationists, and insurance companies, each vying for ownership and salvaging rights to the relics of the ill-fated vessel.

Amid legal complexities and impassioned discussions, R.M.S Titanic Inc. (later renamed Premiere Exhibitions) emerged as a key player by securing salvage rights. This granted them the authority to retrieve artifacts from the *Titanic's* watery grave for global exhibitions. The company flourished during the Titanic mania of the 90s and early 2000s, captivating audiences world-wide with exhibitions that showcased the haunting remnants of the once-grand ship. However, as interest waned following the 100th anniversary of the sinking and the passing of all survivors, R.M.S Titanic Inc. eventually succumbed to bankruptcy in 2016, though it did later manage to reemerge after reorganization, but seemingly not at the same level as before.[145] instead they shifted focus from obtaining artifacts to preserving them. In 2023, R.M.S Titanic inc announced they would suspend until further notice all further artifact recovery missions at the wreck site, following the implosion of the tourist submersible *Titan*.[146]

The submersible *Titan*, operated by the company OceanGate, had met a catastrophic end when it imploded during its descent to the *Titanic* wreck, resulting in the instant loss of all aboard.[147] This incident sent shock waves through the maritime and exploration communities, amplifying concerns over the perils of commercializing the *Titanic* site. The implosion of the *Titan* underscored the dangers inherent in such endeavors, prompting a reevaluation of the balance between exploration, preservation, and the ethical responsibility associated with accessing historical underwater sites.

As the world grappled with the aftermath of the *Titan* tragedy, it became evident that issues beyond mere commercialization had played a role in the submersible's implosion. The incident spurred a renewed commitment to safety standards and respon-

[145] https://www.cnn.com/2020/02/19/us/salvage-company-titanic-radio/index.html

[146] https://www.cbsnews.com/news/titanic-artifacts-plan-canceled-paul-henri-nargeolet-death-submersible-implosion/

[147] https://www.cbsnews.com/news/titan-submersible-implosion-coast-guard-recovers-presumed-human-remains-debris-titanic-wreckage/

sible exploration practices in the fragile depths of the ocean. The complex legacy of the Titanic expanded to encompass not only its historical and emotional significance but also the need for caution and ethical considerations in the pursuit of maritime exploration and preservation. The Titanic, forever a symbol of human ambition and vulnerability, left a lasting impact on the delicate interplay between history, commerce, and the preservation of the past.

Chapter 15

The Third Sister is Born

In the triumphant aftermath of *Olympic*'s maiden voyage in 1911, optimism reigned at Harland and Wolff's Belfast shipyard. The White Star Line's gamble on the Olympic-class trio—a fleet of unprecedented size, luxury, and modernity—was paying off. *Olympic* had launched to great acclaim, swiftly becoming the pride of the North Atlantic and a symbol of British maritime dominance. With the *Titanic* already well into construction, Harland and Wolff turned their attention to the third ship in the series, known during early planning phases simply as "Number 433."

At the time, it was widely assumed that this final sister ship would follow in the established tradition of grandeur set by her predecessors. Early press coverage and speculative commentary suggested that she would be named *Gigantic*—a fitting progression from *Titanic*, and a name fully in line with the White Star Line's pattern of bold, mythic branding. Indeed, several contemporary newspapers, shipping registries, and trade publications referenced the forthcoming liner as the *Gigantic* well into late 1911. Promotional materials surfaced as well, including a now-famous poster touting the vessel under that very name. Although this poster is widely believed not to have originated from the White Star Line directly, its existence reflects just how firmly the name *Gigantic* had entered the public imagination.

Officially, however, neither Harland and Wolff nor the White Star Line ever confirmed the name in formal documents that survive today. There is no evidence that the name *Gigantic* was inscribed on the keel, entered into the company's shipbuilding registers, or used in correspondence beyond informal references. Whether it was a working title, a marketing error, or a discarded naming choice remains a matter of debate among maritime historians.

The first official confirmation of the new ship's name came from *The New York Times* on September 11, 1912, announcing that she would be christened *Britannic*.[148] The choice marked a notable departure from the mythological naming convention and reflected a more grounded, patriotic theme. Rather than projecting the colossal scale of the ship, the name *Britannic* invoked national pride, unity, and strength. It was, perhaps, a conscious pivot—a rhetorical and emotional recalibration in response to the tragedy that had preceded her. What is certain though, is that no actual evidence has been uncovered or made publicly available confirming the name *Gigantic*.

---

[148] https://www.nytimes.com/1912/09/12/archives/to-be-named-britannic-official-announcement-regarding-50000ton.html

Unofficial poster suggesting the third ship would be named Gigantic[149]

"The origin of the poster that you illustrate is extremely vague, but it is quite certain that it was not a piece of official White Star Line publicity. Nor did it have anything to do with Harland and Wolff. What is certain is that as of October 1911, the only name in the available Harland and Wolff records is Britannic. None of the documents at the Public Record Office of Northern Ireland (PRONI) record any name changes even after the vessel had been ordered, which was almost six months before the Titanic went down."

–Simon Mills, Britannic Wreck owner[150]

Whatever name she would ultimately bear, the third of the Olympic-class liners took shape at Harland and Wolff's sprawling shipyard in Belfast. On November 30, 1911, just months before *Titanic*'s ill-fated maiden voyage, the keel of hull number 433 was laid down on Slipway No. 2—the very berth that had hosted the assembly of *Olympic* just a few years prior. At the time, construction proceeded under the confident assumptions that had defined the era: bigger was better, and these ships— protected by watertight compartments and the latest maritime technologies—were considered marvels of engineering, if not virtually unsinkable.

But April 15, 1912, shattered those illusions. The loss of *Titanic*, and the unprecedented scale of the tragedy that fol-

---

[149] https://www.jmilford-titanic.com/2013/10/what-happened-to-gigantic.html

[150] https://www.jmilford-titanic.com/2013/10/what-happened-to-gigantic.html

lowed, cast a long shadow over the future of ocean travel and left the shipping world in a state of reckoning. Overnight, the language of luxury was replaced with a lexicon of safety. Confidence gave way to caution. And the still-forming hull of hull 433—the future *Britannic*—became a canvas upon which an entire industry would attempt to redeem itself.

Though construction had already begun, the ship was still early enough in her build to allow for sweeping design revisions. The most visible and consequential of these was the widening of the vessel's beam—from 92 feet to 94 feet—allowing for the integration of a double hull along the length of her flanks.[151] This change offered greater resistance against underwater breaches while preserving her spacious interiors. It also increased her displacement, requiring a substantial upgrade in her propulsion system.

---

[151] https://www.titanicconnections.com/construction-of-britannic/

Britannic at Harland & Wolff, 1914[152]

Unlike her sisters, *Britannic* was equipped with engines rated at 50,000 shaft horsepower, a notable increase over the 46,000 horsepower systems aboard both *Olympic* and *Titanic*.[153] The upgrade not only compensated for the ship's larger dimensions but also improved maneuverability—an essential feature should she be called upon for non-commercial use, as the looming tensions in Europe made increasingly likely.

Perhaps most critical were the measures taken to improve *Britannic*'s chances of survival in the event of disaster. Lessons from *Titanic* were applied with uncompromising focus. The ship's internal watertight bulkheads were raised significantly—

[152] https://collections.nationalmuseumsni.org/object-hoyfm-hw-h1951

[153] https://www.theshipyardblog.com/hmhs-britannic/

some reaching all the way to B Deck—making it possible for her to remain afloat even with six compartments flooded. *Titanic*, by comparison, could only endure the flooding of four. This adjustment represented not just a technical improvement but a shift in mentality: safety was no longer secondary to luxury. It was the new mandate.

Lifeboat provision saw even more dramatic expansion. *Britannic* was fitted with five massive gantry davits designed by Welin, each capable of handling multiple lifeboats. In total, the ship carried 55 lifeboats, with a total capacity for over 3,600 individuals—more than enough to accommodate her maximum complement of passengers and crew. In an era still reeling from images of empty davits and stranded souls in the North Atlantic, such precautions were both prudent and symbolic: the great liners would no longer fail their charges.

After more than two years of meticulous construction, *Britannic* was launched into the waters of Belfast Lough on February 26, 1914. Thousands of onlookers gathered to watch as the gleaming hull slid down the slipway, a testament to renewed engineering vision and national pride. At 48,158 gross tons, she was the largest of her class—a formidable, modern vessel that embodied both the ambitions and anxieties of a new age.

Following her launch, *Britannic* entered drydock for fitting out, and her builders set about crafting interiors meant to rival, and even surpass, those of her elder sisters. Plans called for an enlarged first-class dining saloon, improved ventilation systems, ornate lounges, and suites that would cater to the most affluent travelers of the transatlantic elite. *Britannic* was envisioned not just as a ship, but as a floating palace—restoring the White Star Line's reputation after the devastating blow dealt by *Titanic*.

But the world had other plans.

Only months after *Britannic*'s launch, Europe was plunged into war. The outbreak of World War I in the summer of 1914 brought peacetime shipbuilding to a halt. Civilian construction slowed to a crawl as national priorities shifted toward the battlefield. At Harland and Wolff, work on *Britannic*'s luxurious interior fittings was suspended. Her hull sat complete, her engines ready—but her ballrooms, lounges, and fine salons remained unfinished, silent testimony to a world suddenly too burdened by conflict to care for elegance.[154]

As the war escalated, her older sister *Olympic* was pressed into service as a troop transport. The Gallipoli campaign, launched in 1915, brought unimaginable casualties, and the British Admiralty soon found itself in urgent need of large, fast vessels capable of carrying wounded soldiers back to England. Though *Britannic* had been built for comfort, her size, speed, and modern medical layout made her an ideal candidate for conversion into a hospital ship.

On November 13, 1915, the Admiralty formally requisitioned *Britannic*.[155] A sweeping transformation began. Her intended splendor was stripped away or reimagined for a new kind of purpose. Lavish dining rooms became medical wards. Grand suites were reconfigured into surgical bays and triage areas. Spaces meant for leisure were adapted into sterilization rooms, dispensaries, and storage for medical equipment. Rather than hosting aristocrats and celebrities, *Britannic* would now carry stretchers, nurses, and the wounded.

The ship's exterior, too, underwent a dramatic rebranding.

---

[154] https://hmhsbritannic.weebly.com/construction.html

[155] https://www.titanicconnections.com/britannics-career/

Her hull was painted white—strikingly different from the dark livery worn by *Olympic* and *Titanic*. A broad green stripe stretched across each side, punctuated by three enormous red crosses. These markings designated her status under the Hague Convention as a hospital ship, affording her protection from attack under international law. Atop her funnels, the White Star buff was replaced with horizontal green bands, further signaling her new humanitarian role to all who saw her at sea.

Thus, *Britannic* emerged not as the opulent successor to *Titanic*, but as something altogether different: a vessel reborn through necessity, charged not with ferrying the wealthy across oceans, but with saving lives in a world tearing itself apart.

She was ready—but her mission would be short-lived.

16

Chapter 16

War Service

The conversion of *Britannic* from a luxury ocean liner into a wartime hospital ship was as swift as it was sobering. Designed to be the crowning jewel of the White Star Line's transatlantic fleet, she had been built with an eye toward opulence—ballrooms adorned with fine wood paneling, first-class suites rivaling the best hotels, dining rooms that echoed with the grandeur of Edwardian high society. But when the British Admiralty requisitioned her on November 13, 1915, the call to arms allowed little time for sentimentality.

Less than three weeks were allotted to overhaul the 48,000-ton vessel for medical service—a monumental task by any measure, let alone amid a war that strained shipyards, materials, and manpower. The urgency was driven by the brutal realities of the Gallipoli campaign, where Allied forces suffered devastating casualties and the need for fast, seaworthy hospital ships had become critical. *Britannic*, with her size, speed, and already-improved safety features, was an obvious candidate.

In dock at Harland and Wolff, ornate interiors intended to rival the splendor of *Olympic* and *Titanic* were rapidly dismantled. Gilded mirrors, mahogany paneling, velvet drapes, and mosaic tiles gave way to antiseptic efficiency. First-class staterooms were stripped and reconfigured as recovery rooms. Lounges were replaced with hospital wards and operating theaters. Public rooms became sterilization areas, isolation wards, and surgical prep stations. When the dust settled, *Britannic* could accommodate an astonishing 3,309 patients—making her one of the largest and most comprehensively equipped hospital ships of the war.

Despite the haste of the conversion, many of the modifications were thoughtfully conceived, leveraging the vessel's generous dimensions. Wide corridors allowed for the easy movement of stretchers and medical carts. Ventilation systems were upgraded to reduce the spread of infection. Her hull—already reinforced with a double bottom and improved watertight bulkheads following the *Titanic* disaster—provided a level of structural safety rarely seen in wartime hospital ships.

Still, compromises were inevitable. While *Britannic* had been outfitted with state-of-the-art Welin-type gantry davits—capable of launching multiple lifeboats simultaneously from a single pivoting arm—not all could be installed in time. The complexity of the system, combined with labor shortages and time constraints, meant that some gantries remained unfinished when she departed. It was a gap in preparedness that would come to bear tragic consequences.

Her outward appearance, too, was transformed to signal her new mission under the protections of international law. In compliance with the Hague Convention, *Britannic*'s hull was painted a stark white, punctuated by a broad green stripe along each side and emblazoned with large red crosses—symbols universally recognized to indicate non-combatant humanitarian service. These visual cues were intended not only to distinguish her from combat vessels, but to grant her immunity from enemy aggression. Her funnels, formerly painted in the distinctive buff-and-black livery of the White Star Line, were ringed in green, completing the ship's rebranding as an instrument of mercy.

H.M.H.S Britannic; Image: the State Library of Victoria

Following this rapid conversion, *Britannic* departed Belfast on December 8, 1915, for her sea trials. Upon successful completion of these initial tests, she proceeded to Liverpool to complete her outfitting and final preparations. Her maiden voyage began just two weeks later, on December 23, 1915. Her destination: the island of Lemnos in the Aegean Sea, which had become a vital medical staging area for casualties evacuated from the Dardanelles during the ill-fated Gallipoli campaign. Interestingly, as Simon Mills[156] of the Titanic Historical Society noted, most of *Britannic's* crew were unaware of their exact destination until well into the voyage—likely a measure taken for operational security.

However, Britannic's rushed conversion did not come without complications. Again, according to Mills, the ship experienced a number of growing pains during her inaugural mission. Faulty valves and improperly sealed portholes allowed water to leak into some of the lower compartments. The situation was compounded by heavy seas and strong winds that battered the ship throughout much of her voyage, causing discomfort for those onboard and raising early concerns about the ship's seaworthiness in her new role.

Despite these early difficulties, *Britannic* pressed on. She made a stop in Naples, Italy, to refuel, before continuing on to Greece. Upon arrival, she took on her first contingent of wounded and sick soldiers. Many of the men, having arrived from the brutal conditions of Gallipoli, were reportedly awestruck by the scale and modernity of *Britannic*, which dwarfed most of the other hospital ships in service at the time.

With her patients secured aboard, *Britannic* began the long journey back to Britain—her immense size, newly assigned purpose, and the red crosses painted on her sides now placing her in stark contrast to the vessel she was originally meant to be.

---

[156] https://titanichistoricalsociety.org/to-hell-and-back-the-maiden-voyage-of-britannic/

* * *

Over the three months in early 1916[157], HMHS *Britannic* performed her duties with quiet efficiency and commendable resilience. In the span of three voyages to the Eastern Mediterranean, she successfully repatriated hundreds of wounded and sick soldiers from the blood-soaked fields of Gallipoli to the relative safety of the United Kingdom. The campaign, marked by bitter terrain, logistical failures, and staggering casualties, had taxed the resources of the British military medical system. *Britannic*, with her immense capacity, modern surgical facilities, and fast transit speeds, became a welcome presence in the Allied evacuation effort.

Despite rough seas and the challenges of her relatively untested conversion, *Britannic* proved herself an exceptional hospital ship. Her large size ensured stability in heavy weather, her upgraded engines maintained reliable schedules, and her spacious wards offered conditions far superior to many other vessels then serving in similar capacities. Praise filtered back from military authorities and medical staff alike: *Britannic* was efficient, reliable, and humane—a vessel fit not for luxury, but for life-saving.

But as the Gallipoli campaign drew to its ignoble end in early 1916, the need for such large-scale medical evacuations sharply declined. The Allied withdrawal was complete by January, and with no immediate deployments requiring her specialized services, *Britannic* was quietly stood down. Her fourth voyage never materialized. Instead, she was withdrawn from active

---

[157] https://atlanticliners.com/white_star_home/britannic_home/

duty and returned to Belfast, where she was berthed under the assumption that her wartime role had concluded.

At Harland and Wolff, her grand civilian identity was revived. Shipwrights and artisans resumed the work they had abandoned during the initial conversion: laying fine wood paneling, fitting crystal chandeliers, installing marble fireplaces and luxury furnishings meant to appeal to the most discerning first-class traveler. Once more, *Britannic* was envisioned as the pinnacle of transatlantic travel—a ship not just of great utility, but of elegance and status, poised to restore the White Star Line's reputation following the catastrophic loss of *Titanic*.

That restoration, however, was to be short-lived.

In the summer of 1916, war erupted anew in the Balkans. The re-ignition of military operations in Greece, Macedonia, and along the Salonika Front created fresh waves of casualties, prompting a renewed demand for hospital ships. The scale and severity of the fighting, combined with outbreaks of disease in the harsh conditions of the Eastern front, once again strained the capacity of existing medical evacuation systems.

On August 28, 1916, *Britannic* was officially requisitioned by the Admiralty for a second time.

Having already undergone one conversion, her return to service was swift. The work carried out in late 1915 provided a blueprint: wards were rapidly reinstalled, surgical theaters reassembled, and operating equipment brought back aboard. Within weeks, she was back in uniform. Her hull was repainted in hospital colors—white with broad green stripes and red crosses—and her crew remobilized. By early September, she was stationed off the Isle of Wight, temporarily serving as a floating hospital where she received wounded soldiers from coastal installations and smaller naval vessels operating in the

Channel.

By September 24, *Britannic* had returned to active Mediterranean service. Her mission was clear and familiar: to transport the injured and ill from the front lines near the Dardanelles and Salonika back to safer ports in Britain. She completed two more round trips in the following weeks, each voyage reflecting the ship's increased efficiency and the crew's hard-earned experience. The process was now smooth and practiced. Medical protocols had been refined, lifeboat drills standardized, and coordination between ship and shore tightened.

By this point, *Britannic* was not only the largest hospital ship in the Royal Navy's fleet but one of the most respected. She had become, in effect, a floating hospital system—able to triage, treat, and stabilize hundreds of patients at a time. Her size allowed for dedicated surgical spaces, wards for infectious disease, recovery areas, and even accommodation for medical personnel and Red Cross volunteers. There were few ships on any side of the conflict that could match her scale or sophistication.

On November 12, 1916, she departed Southampton for what would become her sixth and final voyage.

Her destination was Lemnos, a small Greek island that had become a central hub for Allied operations in the Aegean. The route was well-worn. She had made the crossing several times. Her officers were familiar with the navigational hazards of the area. Her crew had settled into their wartime routines. There was no indication that this journey would differ from those that came before.

And yet, unknowingly, *Britannic* was sailing toward the end of her brief but remarkable life.

In many respects, she was the best-prepared ship of her kind ever to serve in war: she boasted reinforced bulkheads, a double hull, improved lifeboat davits, and state-of-the-art medical facilities. She had learned, structurally and operationally, from the mistakes of *Titanic*. But the seas in which she sailed were not governed by design.

They were governed by chance, by conflict, and by the cold logic of war.

In the early hours of November 21, 1916, less than ten days after her departure from Southampton, *Britannic* would encounter a hidden peril—one that no blueprint or precaution could fully overcome. The youngest and strongest of the Olympic-class sisters would meet a fate eerily reminiscent of her doomed sibling.

Chapter 17

Déjà vu

The fateful sequence of events began on November 17, 1916, when HMHS *Britannic* found herself delayed in the port of Naples, Italy. A series of violent storms sweeping across the Mediterranean had made it too dangerous for the ship to continue her journey toward Greece. Though inconvenient, this enforced pause was ultimately prudent, as the ship's mission was to safely transport injured soldiers. Venturing into treacherous waters under such conditions would have risked far greater disaster.

Captain Charles Bartlett, a seasoned and level-headed offi-cer, used this time wisely, monitoring weather patterns and awaiting a break in the storm. When the winds finally calmed and the seas grew manageable, Bartlett seized the opportunity. On the morning of November 19, Britannic weighed anchor and resumed her course toward the Aegean.[158] Two days later, on November 21, she arrived off the coast of Greece, preparing to embark another group of wounded from the ongoing campaigns in the Balkans.

But tragedy struck with terrifying suddenness.

At precisely 8:12 AM on November 21, as Britannic made her way through the narrow Kea Channel, a thunderous explosion erupted beneath her starboard bow. The jolt was so powerful that it was felt throughout the massive vessel, shuddering through steel bulkheads and echoing like a cannon blast across the surrounding waters. Initial confusion quickly gave way to dread—Britannic had either struck a naval mine or been torpedoed.[159] At the time, the waters around the Greek archipelago were a known danger zone, heavily mined by German U-boats like U-73 as part of their ruthless campaign of unrestricted submarine warfare.

Despite the clear markings of a hospital ship—white hull, green stripe, and bold red crosses—Germany had increasingly targeted such vessels, claiming they were being used to transport munitions or troops. Whether it was a mine or a torpedo, Britannic had now become another casualty of the brutal sea war.

Captain Bartlett acted swiftly and decisively. He immediately ordered the watertight doors to be closed, hoping to contain the flooding and buy precious time. However, six forward compartments had already been breached, as several watertight

---

[158] https://www.westernfrontassociation.com/world-war-i-articles/the-loss-of-the-britannic-21-november-1916/

[159] https://www.upi.com/Archives/1916/11/22/Britannic-victim-of-torpedo-or-mine-in-the-Aegean-Sea/1951511146793/

doors either jammed or failed to seal properly, rendering his efforts ineffective. Unlike her sister *Titanic*, *Britannic* had been designed with additional safety measures, including reinforced bulkheads and a greater number of lifeboats.

These safety features meant that *Britannic* should be able to stay afloat if six of her watertight compartments were flooded. As this was the exact case here, it does beg the question, why did *Britannic* sink anyway? It was in fact, a fateful decision by the ship nurses that dealt the fatal blow to Britannic.

In preparation to taking on injured entity, a series of open portholes along the lower decks were opened by the nursing staff earlier to ventilate the wards in anticipation of receiving patients—allowed water to pour in unchecked.[160] The ship's list increased rapidly, and *Britannic* began to sink by the bow.

Captain Bartlett, realizing the dire situation but unwilling to abandon hope, made a bold decision. Though still over 30 miles from Kea Island, he attempted to beach the massive liner on the nearby coast.[161] His intent was to save the ship and spare the lives of those aboard. But as *Britannic* surged forward under her own power, the flow of seawater into the wounded hull only intensified, accelerating the sinking.

Meanwhile, the lifeboats were being prepared, though Bartlett held off on officially ordering their launch. He understood the danger posed by the ship's still-turning propellers. Unfortunately, his caution was undermined when two lifeboats were launched prematurely by the crew. In the

---

[160] https://www.westernfrontassociation.com/world-war-i-articles/the-loss-of-the-britannic-21-november-1916/

[161] https://www.theguardian.com/world/2008/oct/29/titanic-britannic-marine-museum-sea

ensuing chaos, both boats were drawn into the powerful vortex of the still turning propellers, which were now starting to come above the waterline. The blades shattered the wooden boats and mangled those within, resulting in the deaths of 30 people.[162]

Among the survivors of this grim episode was Violet Jessop, a stewardess-turned-nurse who had earned a reputation as "unsinkable." Remarkably, this was her third brush with maritime catastrophe—she had survived the sinking of *Titanic* in 1912 and the collision of *Olympic* with HMS *Hawke* in 1911. Her escape from *Britannic* would become a legend in its own right.

> "I leapt into the water but was sucked under the ship's keel which struck my head. I escaped, but years later when I went to my doctor because of a lot of headaches, he discovered I had once sustained a fracture of the skull!"[163]
>
> ~ *Violet Jessop*

Violet Jessop's extraordinary escape from the Britannic cemented her unique and almost mythical status in maritime history. With this third brush with death, she became the only known individual to have survived major disasters on

---

[162] https://www.westernfrontassociation.com/world-war-i-articles/the-loss-of-the-britannic-21-november-1916/

[163] https://www.milemarker.co.uk/post/the-unsinkable#:~:text=I%20escaped%2C%20but%20years%20later,solely%20a%20result%20of%20luck.

all three of the Olympic-class liners—*Olympic*, *Titanic*, and *Britannic*. Her presence aboard these doomed vessels seemed almost surreal, and her resilience earned her the nickname "Miss Unsinkable." After the war, Jessop continued working at sea for some years, serving aboard smaller, less renowned ships. Eventually, she retired from maritime life, settling quietly back in England, her incredible story known only to a few at the time.

As the Britannic continued to flood at an alarming rate, Captain Charles Bartlett remained on the bridge, doing everything within his power to stabilize the situation. But by 8:42 AM—just thirty minutes after the explosion—it became clear that the ship could not be beached. The rate of flooding had overwhelmed the forward compartments, and the list was worsening by the minute. Recognizing the inevitability of the ship's loss, Bartlett finally gave the order to abandon ship.

Distress signals had been transmitted earlier, but no response was forthcoming. The crew, growing increasingly desperate, believed that no one was answering their call for help. In truth, the ship's main wireless aerial had been torn down in the explosion, leaving their messages unheard. The *Britannic* was sinking—and she was doing so in silence.

As the water surged higher, rising relentlessly toward the upper decks, Captain Bartlett refused to leave his post until the very last possible moment. By the time the sea reached the bridge, he found himself quite literally wading into the encroaching waters. He swam to a nearby lifeboat, where he resumed overseeing the evacuation and coordinated rescue efforts.[164]

---

[164] https://web.archive.org/web/20090806070941/http://www.titanic-tita nic.com/britannic.shtml

By now, the decks of the *Britannic* were nearly submerged, and those left aboard scrambled to reach lifeboats or jump into the water. Nurses, doctors, and crew-members worked tirelessly to aid the wounded and guide passengers to safety, even as the ship groaned under the weight of her mortal wounds. Lifeboats, both launched and drifting, filled the sea, carrying survivors away from the dying giant.

At 9:07 AM, just 55 minutes after the explosion, Britannic succumbed to her fate. Her bow, already submerged, struck the ocean floor with a deafening, bone-rattling crash, despite the water being only about 400 feet deep—shallow for a vessel that stretched 883 feet in length.[165] The sudden halt caused the stern to rear slightly before beginning its final descent.

A deep, eerie creaking echoed across the Aegean as the ship's steel hull twisted under the strain. The Britannic then rolled slowly onto her starboard side, driven by the water already inside and the open portholes that had sealed her doom. In a matter of seconds, the last visible part of her—the towering funnels and the stern—vanished beneath the surface. The sea fell silent again, save for the scattered cries of survivors.

Out of the roughly 1,100 people onboard that morning, 30 tragically lost their lives, having been killed when the two lifeboats were pulled into the still-spinning propellers early in the evacuation. Though the number of fatalities was far lower than the Titanic disaster four years earlier, the circumstances were no less harrowing.

Roughly an hour after the sinking, two British naval vessels,

---

[165] https://www.pbs.org/lostliners/britannic.html#:~:text=The%20Britann ic%20sank%20in%20only,had%20interrupted%20a%20routine%20m orning.

the HMS *Scourge* and HMS *Heroic,* arrived on the scene, guided by the plumes of smoke and the reports from other nearby ships. They began pulling survivors from the water and lifting overcrowded lifeboats aboard. Many of the doctors and nurses from Britannic, though shaken and soaked, resumed their duties without hesitation, tending to the wounded even in the aftermath of their own trauma.

Additional vessels soon joined the rescue operation, helping to ferry the survivors back to medical facilities and eventually home to England. For those who lived through it, the sinking of the Britannic would forever remain etched in memory—an experience marked by chaos, courage, and immense loss.

Chapter 18

A Forgotten Legacy

When the First World War came to a merciful end in 1918, the landscape of Europe was unrecognizable. The Austro-Hungarian and Ottoman empires—once cornerstones of continental power—had collapsed into fractured successor states. The German Empire was dismantled, replaced by a fragile republic. Russia, in the throes of civil war, had descended into violent revolution. The trauma of mechanized warfare had scarred every corner of the continent, leaving millions dead, and millions more displaced.

In such a moment of epochal upheaval, the loss of a single ship—even one as grand as HMHS *Britannic*—barely registered in the public consciousness. She was but one of more than 6,000 vessels sunk during the war. And though her end was sudden and tragic, it unfolded within the wider cadence of global catastrophe. Amid the trenches of the Western Front and the blockades of the Atlantic, *Britannic*'s story became just another thread in the tangle of wartime destruction.

Yet to dismiss her loss as merely statistical would be to overlook a deeper truth. For though *Britannic* never fulfilled her intended role as a premier transatlantic liner, and though her death was eclipsed by the far greater horror surrounding her, her legacy is both distinct and enduring.

Unlike the *Titanic*, whose sinking reverberated through peacetime society and galvanized public outrage, *Britannic*'s demise generated little fanfare. Her role—as a hospital ship in active service—meant her loss was folded into the routine tragedies of war. There were no international commissions convened in the aftermath. No banner headlines accusing her captain or design flaws. No sweeping cultural reckoning. Her wreck was recorded, investigated in summary fashion, and then left to rest.

Captain Charles Bartlett[166], unlike the ill-fated Captain Edward Smith of *Titanic*, was spared public scrutiny. There were no sensationalist calls for justice, no personal vilification. Instead, *Britannic* was cataloged as an unfortunate casualty of maritime warfare—likely struck by a German mine, possibly even a torpedo, though the debate lingered for decades. Whatever the truth, she became a symbol not of scandal, but of the impersonal cruelty of conflict: a vessel built for beauty and comfort, repurposed for mercy, and ultimately undone by the indiscriminate instruments of war.

In fact, *Britannic* holds a tragic distinction that sets her apart. At 48,158 gross tons, she remains the largest ship sunk during

---

[166] http://www.titanictown.plus.com/titanictown/britannic.htm

World War I.[167] It is a record that few remember—and none would ever wish to claim.

Yet the name *Britannic* did not sink with her into the silted floor of the Aegean.

In 1930, more than a decade after the war's end, the White Star Line christened a new vessel: MV *Britannic*[168], a motor liner designed for the revived transatlantic trade. Unlike her predecessor, this *Britannic* was smaller, sleeker, and more modern—built in an era defined less by glamour and more by economic uncertainty. The Great Depression loomed. The opulence of the Edwardian age had faded. Ocean liners, once symbols of imperial prowess and industrial supremacy, now competed for efficiency and survival.

Nevertheless, the name carried weight. It was a name already laden with memory—a name that evoked grandeur, loss, and duty. Though the new *Britannic* bore no structural or design relation to the Olympic-class trio, she could not escape the legacy of the shipwreck that preceded her. Every departure carried a silent passenger: remembrance.

When global war returned in 1939, the new *Britannic* once again traded luxury for necessity. Requisitioned by the British government during the Second World War, she served as a troopship, ferrying thousands of soldiers across dangerous waters. Unlike her namesake, however, she survived. She emerged from the war with honor, having carried over 180,000 troops during her service[169]—an unsung lifeline of logistics

---

[167] https://uboat.net/wwi/ships_hit/largest.html

[168] https://whitestarmoments.wixsite.com/whitestarmoments/mv-britannic
-1

[169] https://greatships.net/britannic3

and perseverance.

MV Britannic

In peacetime, she returned to civilian service, completing her career with quiet determination. She weathered changing fashions, shifting routes, and a rapidly evolving transportation industry. But by the 1950s and 60s, the age of the ocean liner was nearing its end. Jet aircraft had begun to dominate transatlantic travel. Romance and ritual were no match for speed and economy.

In 1960, after three decades of service, the new *Britannic* was sold to scrappers. There was no ceremony. No commemorative voyage. She was quietly dismantled, her steel torn down and sold—another relic of an era that had passed into history. Her end was peaceful, but it was final. With her, the White Star

Line's last surviving namesake of the Olympic-class vision was gone.

And yet, *Britannic* endures.

Not in steel. Not in steam. But in story.

The first *Britannic*, resting beneath the Aegean, remains one of the best-preserved shipwrecks of the early 20th century. She lies as both a war grave and a time capsule—her corridors flooded but recognizable, her design still testifying to the ambitions of her builders. Protected by international agreement, she is a solemn reminder of the lives lost and the service rendered during a war that reshaped the world.

Her story, once muted by the noise of greater calamities, has been gradually rediscovered by divers, historians, and maritime enthusiasts. No longer merely "*Titanic*'s sister," *Britannic* has emerged as a figure of historical significance in her own right—a ship whose journey was marked by transformation, adaptation, and quiet sacrifice.

Even the second *Britannic*, though less famous, contributed to the name's evolving legacy. Her successful wartime service and dignified civilian career represent the other side of maritime history—not the dramatic sinking, but the endurance; not the icon, but the worker.

Taken together, these two ships bearing the name *Britannic* form a continuum. They speak not just to the triumphs and tragedies of their respective eras, but to the shifting nature of remembrance itself. The grandeur of ocean liners, once so central to national identity and technological pride, has faded. But the stories they carried—the lives they touched—remain.

In the final analysis, *Britannic* represents more than maritime engineering or wartime logistics. She embodies the fragility of even our most magnificent creations, and the enduring human desire to make meaning from loss. Her legacy, obscured for decades, now flickers again in the currents of memory.

While *Titanic* may forever occupy the center stage of cultural fascination, *Britannic* waits just beyond the spotlight—a quieter figure in the same mythic family, a silent witness to the tides of war, peace, and progress. Her name is still spoken—not in mourning, but in respect.

And in that continued remembrance, she sails on.

19

Chapter 19

Sister Discovered

For nearly six decades, the HMHS *Britannic* lay untouched in the quiet depths of the Aegean Sea. Entombed in sediment and secrecy, the final sister of the Olympic-class trio rested in darkness, unseen and largely unstudied—her story obscured by the twin veils of time and myth. While the tragic sinking of *Titanic* in 1912 had become a defining moment in modern memory, and *Olympic* had earned distinction through longevity and wartime service, *Britannic* remained a spectral figure in maritime history—known more by association than by her own merits.

That silence was finally broken in 1975.

It was in that year that world-renowned explorer Jacques Cousteau[170] led a diving expedition to locate and examine the

_____

[170] https://www.britannica.com/topic/Britannic

wreck of *Britannic*. By then, Cousteau had already revolutionized undersea exploration and filmmaking, bringing the mysteries of the ocean to a global audience. His interest in the lost hospital ship marked a significant turning point—not only for public awareness of *Britannic*, but for maritime archaeology more broadly.

Cousteau's team located the ship just off the Greek island of Kea, lying on her starboard side at a depth of approximately 120 meters (roughly 400 feet). What they discovered was far more than a wreck—it was a remarkably preserved artifact of World War I, frozen in time. Despite the devastating explosion that led to her sinking in November 1916, *Britannic*'s hull remained largely intact. Her stern towered above the seafloor. Her corridors, though dark and corroded, still contained traces of their original function. In contrast to *Titanic*, whose grave lies two and a half miles beneath the icy North Atlantic and whose remains are fragmented and fragile, *Britannic* appeared almost serene.

The preservation of the wreck is due in large part to the conditions of the Aegean. Warmer waters, lower pressure, and minimal ocean current helped preserve the ship's structural features and contents. For researchers, this offered a rare opportunity: to study a major 20th-century shipwreck up close and in situ, with relatively little degradation. For the public, Cousteau's footage and findings offered a haunting glimpse into a lesser-known maritime disaster—one that echoed the grandeur and tragedy of *Titanic*, but with its own story to tell.

Cousteau's initial dives also reopened old questions. Early reports speculated that *Britannic* might have been sunk by a German torpedo, rather than by a naval mine. This theory, if true, would have represented a serious violation of international law, as *Britannic* was clearly marked and registered as a hospital ship. However, as further explorations took place in the 1980s and 1990s—led by British and Greek teams in cooperation with maritime historians and forensic analysts—a clearer picture began to emerge.

The damage patterns observed along the bow were consistent not with a torpedo impact, but with the explosion of a mine— an underwater charge laid by German forces to disrupt Allied supply and hospital routes. The area in which *Britannic* sank had been mined weeks earlier by the German U-boat *U-73*, making it likely that the ship's hull struck one of these submerged weapons during her outbound voyage to pick up the wounded from Salonika. The mine exploded beneath the forward hold, causing extensive flooding and disabling critical bulkheads. Despite swift evacuation efforts, the ship sank in less than an hour, taking 30 lives.

The tragedy was compounded by the fact that many of those who perished did so not from the explosion itself, but during the attempted launch of lifeboats while the ship's engines were still running. Several lifeboats were drawn into the propellers, a mistake that proved fatal. Still, the majority of those aboard— over 1,000 crew and medical personnel—survived, a testament to improved safety measures implemented after *Titanic*'s loss.

In the years following Cousteau's discovery, interest in *Britannic* gradually expanded. Historians and documentarians returned to the site, conducting more detailed surveys using sonar, remote-operated vehicles, and underwater photography. These efforts have helped clarify not only the circumstances of the ship's sinking, but also her operational role as a hospital ship. Archival research and dive-based investigations have confirmed that *Britannic* carried no contraband, no weapons, and no munitions—a direct refutation of German wartime claims designed to justify unrestricted submarine warfare.

As such, her sinking is recognized not only as a military loss, but as a humanitarian tragedy.

Today, the wreck of *Britannic* is protected by both British and Greek authorities, classified as a war grave under international agreements. Access is strictly limited to professional divers with permits, and exploration is conducted under guidelines that ensure respect for the site and for those who lost their lives. She is not a destination for recreational diving or commercial salvage. She is a resting place.

The rediscovery of *Britannic* has contributed to a larger reevaluation of her historical legacy. Once dismissed as merely "*Titanic*'s sister," she is now recognized as a vessel of significant historical value in her own right. She was the most technically advanced of the Olympic-class liners, incorporating many safety features that would become standard in the years after 1912. She served as a hospital ship at a time when medicine and warfare were undergoing radical change. And she carried with her not just patients, but the hopes of a world desperately trying to heal amid chaos.

Britannic's memory is preserved not only in documentaries and dive logs, but in a broader understanding of the human cost of war and the silent dignity of service. In a sense, her story mirrors that of countless lives altered or erased by global conflict—quiet, uncelebrated, but no less worthy of remembrance.

As the Aegean Sea continues to move gently above her, *Britannic* endures—not in grandeur or fame, but in legacy. She reminds us that history is often found not in the loudest stories, but in those discovered patiently, quietly, and with care.

Chapter 20

The Forgotten Sister

After the First World War, Germany was compelled under the Treaty of Versailles to surrender key assets to the Allied powers as reparations for the damage inflicted during the conflict. Among these was the *Bismarck*, a partially completed ocean liner intended for the Hamburg America Line. She was transferred to the United Kingdom, completed by the White Star Line, and renamed *Majestic*. Her addition to the British fleet was intended to compensate for wartime losses—including that of *Britannic*, the third and youngest of the Olympic-class liners.

While *Titanic* would become the most famous ship in maritime history, and *Olympic* enjoyed a long and successful career in both commercial and military service, *Britannic* remained curiously overlooked. Constructed as the improved successor to *Titanic*, *Britannic* was designed with enhanced safety features including reinforced watertight compartments and expanded lifeboat accommodations. Yet she would never carry a single paying passenger.

Commissioned in 1914 and completed the following year, *Britannic* was immediately requisitioned by the British Admiralty before she could begin commercial voyages. As the war intensified, the need for medical evacuation from the Eastern Mediterranean grew urgent. *Britannic* was stripped of her luxurious interiors and converted into His Majesty's Hospital Ship (HMHS) *Britannic*. In this new role, she served not as a vessel of leisure, but as a mobile hospital, equipped to transport the wounded from campaigns such as Gallipoli and Salonika.

The ship's transformation was emblematic of a broader shift in maritime purpose during wartime. Her grand dining rooms became hospital wards; her smoking lounges, surgical stations. The acoustic elegance of her intended voyage across the North Atlantic was replaced by the subdued rhythm of medical care and military routine. *Britannic* carried doctors, nurses, stretcher-bearers, and wounded men across seas now filled with hidden threats.

This shift from commercial ambition to humanitarian mission placed *Britannic* in a distinct historical category. Unlike *Titanic*, whose tragic loss has been endlessly examined and dramatized, *Britannic*'s story remained tethered to her utility and wartime service. Her demise, though tragic, was not cloaked in mystery or myth. On November 21, 1916, while transiting the Kea Channel in the Aegean Sea, *Britannic* struck a German naval mine. Despite the ship's modern safety features and a more experienced crew, she sank within 55 minutes.

Yet the death toll—30 lives lost out of more than 1,000 aboard—was significantly lower than that of her sister. Many of the lessons from the *Titanic* disaster, particularly regarding

lifeboat deployment and evacuation readiness, were implemented effectively. Nevertheless, a critical error during the
sinking resulted in several lifeboats being launched too early,
only to be pulled into the still-revolving propellers. Most
fatalities were among those in these early-launched boats.

In the decades that followed, *Britannic*'s memory lingered
primarily in the shadows. Popular histories tended to focus on
her more famous sibling, whose opulent accommodations and
tragic maiden voyage captured the public imagination. *Olympic*,
with her distinguished record and eventual scrapping in the
1930s, received her share of retrospective attention. *Britannic*,
by contrast, became an historical footnote—referenced in
context but rarely examined in full.

It was not until the late 20th century that *Britannic* began to
receive renewed scholarly and popular interest. Underwater
expeditions located the wreck in 1975, lying on her starboard
side in relatively shallow Aegean waters, remarkably intact
compared to *Titanic*. Jacques Cousteau's 1976 documentary
brought the first images of the ship to public view. Yet it was
not until the cultural wave following James Cameron's 1997
Titanic film that interest surged again.

In 2000, a made-for-television film titled *Britannic* dramatized the ship's final voyage. However, the production took
significant liberties with historical fact, suggesting sabotage
and conspiracy theories long discredited by experts. Despite
strong production values, the film failed to elevate *Britannic*'s
story to the level of her sisters. Instead, it contributed to further
confusion between historical record and fiction, and ultimately
did little to cement *Britannic*'s place in the public consciousness.

What continues to distinguish *Britannic* is not the drama of
her demise, but the dignity of her mission. She was a ship

born into war, repurposed for healing rather than profit. In this role, she ferried thousands of wounded men across hostile waters and brought vital medical services to the front lines of a global conflict. The circumstances of her service and sinking reflect broader themes in early 20th-century maritime history—namely the intersection of technology, warfare, and humanitarian need.

Her story also exemplifies how safety reforms, driven by tragedy, can have lasting impact. *Britannic* incorporated lifeboat improvements, enhanced bulkhead design, and internal communication systems that were direct responses to *Titanic*'s failure. Yet her loss also demonstrated that even these measures were not infallible in the chaos of war.

Today, *Britannic* lies preserved beneath the Aegean Sea, a time capsule of World War I maritime engineering. Protected as a British war grave, she is occasionally visited by divers and continues to be studied by marine archaeologists. For those willing to look beyond the headlines and myths of more famous liners, *Britannic* offers a quieter, more complex legacy—one of resilience, compassion, and adaptation in a world torn by upheaval.

In the broader narrative of ocean liner history, *Britannic* deserves more than to be remembered as merely *Titanic*'s sister. She was a vessel with a purpose distinct from both *Olympic* and *Titanic*, and her service, though brief, was meaningful. As a hospital ship, a product of engineering progress, and a casualty of global conflict, *Britannic* represents the often-overlooked dimension of maritime history: not just the grandeur of transatlantic travel, but the ships that quietly served and sacrificed far from the public eye.

Afterwards

The allure of the *Titanic* and her sister ships endures—resilient, enigmatic, and woven into the fabric of modern mythology. To regard their stories as concluded would be to misunderstand the nature of historical fascination. These ships do not merely inhabit the past; they *haunt* it. They challenge us to look backward not just in remembrance, but in search of meaning— across steel hulls and shattered dreams, through triumphs in engineering and failures in foresight.

There is something ineffable about the Olympic-class liners that continues to captivate, long after their physical forms have vanished or fallen silent beneath the waves. Is it the scale of the tragedy that binds us so tightly to them? Or is it the romanticism—the ornate excess of the Edwardian era, the gleam of polished brass and mahogany, the idea of a gilded age gliding effortlessly across the sea? The answer remains elusive. Perhaps it lies not in one or the other, but in their synthesis: a tragic romance, a reflection of humanity's dual capacity for greatness and hubris.

Each of the three sisters carried within her the spirit of an age. *Olympic*, the stalwart elder, exemplified endurance and reliability—a vessel that adapted, served through war, and retired with dignity. *Titanic*, the ill-fated middle child, became a symbol of ambition undone by nature, remembered not only for how she sank but for what she represented: a dream disrupted. And *Britannic*, the youngest, answered the call of duty rather than luxury, a ship transformed by war and defined by sacrifice. Together, they form a trilogy of human endeavor—one of resilience, tragedy, and quiet heroism.

Their legacy extends far beyond their physical constructions. The *Titanic* disaster triggered sweeping reforms in maritime safety—mandatory lifeboat capacity, international ice patrols, wireless communication protocols, and better emergency preparedness. *Britannic* further tested these improvements under the pressures of war. Even *Olympic* contributed, ferrying troops and surviving attacks, reinforcing the importance of versatility in ship design. These were not merely ships; they were turning points.

Yet their stories are not just technical milestones—they are deeply human narratives. These ships carried emigrants chasing new lives, aristocrats clinging to old worlds, crew members whose lives were shaped by the rhythms of transatlantic service, and families whose fates became entwined with riveted steel and churning waters. In studying the Olympic-class liners, we engage with more than metal and blueprints. We confront questions of class, technology, aspiration, and mortality.

That is why the fascination does not fade. New generations discover these stories and find in them something that speaks to their own age: the limits of certainty, the price of innovation, the tension between nature and progress. Documentaries are still made. Artifacts are still unearthed. Fictional retellings continue to reimagine what was lost. And beneath it all, the truth of these ships persists—layered, enduring, incomplete.

As historians, writers, and curious minds return again and again to these vessels, they are not merely seeking facts. They are listening for echoes—across Atlantic winds and Aegean depths, across decades and disciplines. The *Titanic*, *Olympic*, and *Britannic* remain powerful symbols precisely because they resist easy definition. They remind us that progress is fragile, that ambition must be tempered by humility, and that in every great undertaking there lies the potential for both splendor and sorrow.

In the end, the legacy of these ships is not frozen in 1912 or 1916 or 1935. It lives on—in maritime law, in museums, in film reels, and in the hearts of those who seek to understand the human condition through the lens of these remarkable vessels. They are not simply relics of a bygone era. They are mirrors held up to our own.

And as long as there are questions to be asked and seas to be crossed, the stories of the Olympic-class liners will never truly be over.

About the Author

Joseph Boro is an enthusiastic admirer of History, having gotten his bachelors degree in the subject at the University of Central Florida. He hopes to emphasize his love of history by bringing it to the common person, and get other interested in the subject.

Also by Joseph Boro

The Two Presidents
In "The Two Presidents" by Joseph Boro,
delve into a riveting alternate history
where the course of the world is altered by
the enigmatic Fredrick Mason, an advisor
to President Franklin Roosevelt.

Set against the backdrop of World War II,
this gripping tale poses the intriguing question:

What if?

www.ingramcontent.com/pod-product-compliance
Lightning Source LLC
Chambersburg PA
CBHW011215120626
46545CB00008B/2996

9 789898 985928